Euthanasia: The Heart
of the Matter

Euthanasia:
The Heart of
the Matter

Andrew Dunnett

Hodder & Stoughton
LONDON SYDNEY AUCKLAND

British Library Cataloguing in Publication Data
A record for this book is available from the British Library

ISBN 0 340 69486 6

Typeset by Avon Dataset Ltd, Bidford-on-Avon, Warks

Printed and bound in Great Britain by
The Guernsey Press Co. Ltd, Channel Isles

Hodder & Stoughton Ltd
A Division of Hodder Headline PLC
338 Euston Road
London NW1 3BH

To B.J.M.

Contents

Acknowledgments

I am grateful to all those who gave of their time and indeed their hospitality in order for me to produce this small contribution to the current euthanasia debate. I have fond memories of our discussions, from the Royal Gallery in the House of Lords to the newsroom of the *Observer* and the café at Rotterdam Central railway station. I am grateful to you all for fitting me into your busy and hectic schedules.

To the reader. This is not intended as an intellectual tome, a fact that should be readily clear. I have sought to be journalistic in style and focused on some of the contemporary legal and ethical problems. I hope that, to all who have an interest in the subject, it gives a clear indication of the arguments on an issue that is likely to be the leading ethical debate of the next decade. I have tried to be up front with the issues; I hope you are not disappointed.

Andrew Dunnett
October 1998

About the Author

Andrew Dunnett studied ethics at Durham University prior to working as an advisor to a number of Parliamentarians and corporate social responsibility programmes. He has a keen interest in politics and social affairs and continues to work as a communications advisor to a large number of individuals and groups. He is currently leading the ambitious project to rebuild St Ethelburga's church in the City of London, which was partially destroyed by a terrorist bomb, as a centre for reconciliation and peace.

Foreword

Death is the only certainty in life. It has been said that its contemplation is faced with equanimity only by those who have Wordsworth's 'Faith that looked through death' and by those who claim no faith at all. At the extremes of response to death are those who dedicate their lives to preparing for it and, conversely, those who are content with Juvenal's 'bread and circuses'.

For most of us, however, there is a yearning to reconcile the earliest quest for a full and useful life with our ultimate impotence to sustain it. The dilemma is most acute for those who accept special responsibility for the lives of others and for the nature of their deaths. Doctors, nurses, carers and ministers of religion would be negligent if they were not constantly concerned to contribute to as gentle and easy a death as possible – the original meaning of euthanasia – a word which has fallen victim to the etymological barbarians. It would also be unnatural if those closest to the dying person did not have strong views about 'the intentional killing of a patient by act or omission as part of their medical treatment', as euthanasia is now defined. Likewise it would be strange if lawyers and judges were not to be obliged to take a view about the legality of a death in such circumstances, however merciful the intent, or if philosophers were not concerned with such matters as meaning and quality of life.

However, the issues raised by cases such as patients in persistent or permanent vegetative state (PVS) – of which the tragic young football fan, Tony Bland, is a crucial example – do not concern only their family, friends and professional carers. They concern everyone. It could be us or our loved one who is struck down without warning. Even those who have not given such issues as the withdrawal of basic nutrition any serious thought instinctively know and care that the kind of society in which we and generations still unborn will live, will be influenced for good or ill by the way in which such dilemmas are resolved.

There is no shortage of learned texts for the cognoscenti. But where, until now, is the book for everyone? A book which deals not in philosophical abstractions but in concrete examples, not in professional jargon, but in everyday language. A book which aims to inform, possibly to disturb, but certainly to stimulate wide public debate. A book which compels the reader to work and inwardly digest the whole wide spectrum of views on this most controversial of subjects presented by ten of the most significant figures in the field, and which challenges our individual and collective consciences in a most salutary way.

The author's method is disarmingly simple: question and answer. As any experienced interviewee knows, the quality of the answers depends on the quality of the questions. Mr Dunnett has the rare gift of posing the questions which the reader would have wished to ask, and with just the right touch and tone to evoke responses which ring true, particularly when they are honestly evasive or when the subject unguardedly wraps personal prejudice in a dissembling cloak of principle.

The last year of the old millennium will shape precept and practice in the UK and elsewhere for the new millennium. As the book goes to press, test cases against doctors are imminent and the BMA is again engaging in wide debate. It is safe to predict that this sensitive and engrossing work will be extensively mined by prospectors of the treacherous terrain it covers.

Sir Sandy Macara
ex-Chairman of Council of the BMA

Introduction

The debate surrounding the practice of euthanasia has intensified in the last decade, both in this country and abroad.
Euthanasia is not a new subject, having been debated since
the time of Hippocrates. However, the intensified debate
has been caused by a number of recent developments. The
advance in healthcare technology means that more people
are living longer than ever before, whereas in the past they
would have died at a much earlier stage of an illness. While
this has resulted in many enjoying a prolonged life, there are
some who feel that the poor quality of life arising out of
advanced medical science is more of a burden than a benefit.

At the same time as healthcare technology has advanced,
the relationship between doctors and patients is also changing. In the past the 'doctor knows best' syndrome was often
the style of healthcare practice. Consent was required,
but the relationship was often paternalistic, with the doctor
taking the lead. In the current age of personal autonomy most
patients now wish to be more involved in medical decision-
making. This has resulted in changes in healthcare practice
and in the approach of the doctor.

This debate has been fuelled by pressure-group politics in
the form of a worldwide network of pro-euthanasia groups.
Beginning in the United States but now with groups and
supporters in many countries throughout the world, the 'right
to die' lobby is growing in numbers and in the quality of its
pressure politics. Their activities are being enthusiastically

reported by a media which is interested in 'progress' rather than in maintaining the status quo. Details of the activities of Dr Jack Kervorkian in the USA and Dr Nitschke in Australia make excellent copy in broadsheets as well as tabloids. In contrast, stories regarding hospice care lack the interest needed in the highly competitive media environment.

As a result of these factors a host of important international developments have taken place. In Australia, the Northern Territory, which has a population of 150,000, voted euthanasia into law on 25 May 1995. The Rights of the Terminally Ill Act was subsequently overturned, but not before Dr Nitschke had euthanised his patient Bob Dent. In the United States of America a series of state-wide referenda have been taking place throughout the 1990s in Washington, California and Oregon. In the latter, a measure was passed by 53 per cent to 47 per cent giving patients with six months or less to live the right to ask the attending doctors for drugs to end their lives. However, activities in the USA have focused on retired Michigan pathologist Jack Kervorkian, who by 1996 had killed approximately forty patients. Prosecutions against Dr Kervorkian have failed so many times that it is unlikely that he will be convicted for his activities.

As Australia and the United States look towards legalising euthanasia, the Netherlands has been practising it since the 1980s even though it remains illegal in statute. Following a series of court cases in the 1970s and 1980s, Dutch doctors were exempted from prosecution where certain criteria were met, such as where the patient's request was voluntary and persistent and where the situation was deemed hopeless. In 1993 the Dutch Parliament considered voluntary euthanasia and gave statutory backing to doctors practising it on patients who were suffering a perpetual, unbearable and hopeless situation. The new law does not formally legalise euthanasia and it remains a criminal offence in the penal code, but doctors are now widely practising it in the Netherlands.

While these international developments occurred, the debate was also progressing significantly, if not quite so dramatically, in the United Kingdom. In 1988 the BMA set up a working party to review their guidance on euthanasia, while the Church of England produced its own report, entitled *On Dying Well*. It was the trial of Dr Nigel Cox in 1992 which re-ignited the debate on the subject in the United Kingdom. Dr Cox was later convicted for the attempted murder of his patient Mrs Lilian Boyes after he had administered a lethal dose which had the effect of shortening her life. The case caused dramatic media reporting in the United Kingdom and opinions seemed to be divided in two camps. Some considered Dr Cox to be a medical hero who had acted in accordance with the wishes of his patient and her family and had mercifully treated her with the effect of shortening her life. Others believed that he had breached the ethical code of his profession, and were concerned that, despite having broken the law, he merely received a suspended sentence and the condemnation of the General Medical Council.

Before the debate could subside, the case of Tony Bland was making headlines and creating further controversy in Britain. Tony Bland, a young man severely injured in the Hillsborough football disaster in 1989, was in the condition known as a persistent vegetative state as a result of a lack of oxygen to his brain. His doctor requested the permission of the court to withdraw the provision of nutrition and hydration, which would have the effect of shortening Mr Bland's life. The case would make medical history because, until the judgment, the provision of nutrition and hydration through whatever means had been seen as part of basic nursing care which could not be withdrawn unless the patient was close to death. The case was heard by the Family Division of the High Court and proceeded to the House of Lords, where their Lordships ruled in favour of withdrawing Mr Bland's nutrition and hydration with effect that he subsequently died.

The British media followed the debate with interest and varying degrees of accuracy. Some commentators were adamant that this was the first case of legalised euthanasia while others saw a comparison with the switching off of a life-support machine.

Following the Bland judgment, a number of the Law Lords suggested that Parliament should consider the matter and the House of Lords established a Select Committee on Medical Ethics in 1993, formed to consider the issues raised both by the Cox case and the Bland judgment and by the wider international developments. The Committee was chaired by Lord Walton of Detchant, the eminent neurologist, and included such notable figures as Professor the Lord McColl of Dulwich, the former Archbishop of York Lord Habgood, Baroness Warnock and the former Health Minister Baroness Jay. After a year of activity the Committee unanimously reported that there should be no change in law with regard to euthanasia. While this was a significant setback for those actively campaigning for euthanasia in the United Kingdom, it was not in any sense the final word on the matter.

The debate in the United Kingdom has recently been progressing in the courts with a number of difficult cases being regularly considered by the Family Division of the High Court, most notably the recent case of Annie Lindsell. Lindsell was a sufferer from motor neurone disease who went to the High Court over treatment that could be permitted when the disease was advanced.

It is important at the start to define clearly what is meant by the word 'euthanasia'. Its original and literal translation is 'a gentle and easy death'; however, in recent years the most embracing definition is 'the intentional killing of a patient by act or omission as part of their medical treatment'. This definition embraces active euthanasia, where a healthcare professional takes a course of action, perhaps administering barbiturates or morphine in sufficient quantities to cause respiratory failure, thereby accelerating death.

It also embraces so-called 'passive euthanasia', a term which causes much debate. Passive euthanasia has been used to describe the withholding of treatment which would be necessary for the continuation of the patient's life. Western medical tradition holds the belief that not all possible steps have to be taken to keep a patient alive for as long as possible. The withdrawal or withholding of treatment is acceptable where persistent treatment would be of no benefit to the patient. Western medical tradition sees this as morally acceptable and as good medical practice.

Some consider that passive euthanasia includes the so-called 'principle of double effect'. This is where a doctor prescribes or administers a palliative (pain relief) in the knowledge that a foreseeable but unintended consequence of his action is the shortening of the patient's life. Again, Western medical tradition would not see this as a form of euthanasia but rather as good medical practice, the intention of the doctor being to treat the pain rather than to kill the patient. This principle of double effect, which has been the cause of considerable debate in the UK, will be explored in depth in a later chapter.

Euthanasia can of course come in various forms. It can be voluntary, whereby the patient is free, well informed and able to make their own decision requesting euthanasia. It can be non-voluntary, where a patient is not in a position to understand their circumstances; they may be mentally incapacitated, and therefore cannot exercise their judgment requesting or withholding consent. Euthanasia may also be involuntary, where a patient is competent to request or consent to euthanasia but does not do so and is intentionally killed.

With euthanasia meaning different things to different people, it is not surprising that a considerable amount of debate is steeped in confusion. Indeed, when establishing a Select Committee in 1993 to consider the issue, the House of

Lords decided that the Committee would benefit from the title of 'Medical Ethics' rather than 'Euthanasia'.

During the course of the interviews and accompanying text, a number of terms are used which, while familiar to those who have followed the debate closely, may be new to others. The following are some of the more frequently used terms.

Persistent vegetative state (PVS): A condition in which the brain expresses no evidence of activity in the cerebral cortex, the cognitive part of the brain.

Brain stem death: The condition whereby an individual cannot live without artificial support and ventilation. Once the respirator stops, the heart will stop beating.

Advance directive: A document by which individuals express what treatment they would or would not like in the event of them becoming mentally incapacitated.

Double effect: The principle by which doctors increase the dose of pain relief for patients, with the foreseen but un-intended effect of shortening life.

Palliative care: The system of care as pioneered by the hospice movement which includes the relief of pain and all other active care provided to a patient when the illness is deemed terminal.

Competent patients: Those patients who are able to under-stand the information about their condition and make an informed decision.

Incompetent patients: Those patients who are unable, whether temporarily or permanently, to make decisions about their medical care.

The Mental Incapacity Report: A consultation launched in 1997 by the Lord Chancellor, Lord Irvine, which included discussion of the use of advance directives and the withdrawal of food and fluid from patients in PVS.

The Bland judgment: The decision by the House of Lords which granted permission to the medical staff to withdraw food and water from Tony Bland, injured in the Hillsborough football tragedy.

The Cox case: The trial of Dr Nigel Cox took place in 1992. Dr Cox was convicted of attempted murder following administering a lethal dose to a suffering patient.

The Lindsell case: A sufferer from motor neurone disease who went to the High Court in 1997 over treatment that could be permitted when the disease advanced.

The Chabot case: A prosecution brought in the Netherlands against a Dutch doctor who administered a fatal injection to a woman suffering from severe depression.

The Remmelink Report: A Dutch government report, published in 1991, concerning the practice of euthanasia in the Netherlands.

Dr Philip Nitschke

Biographical details

Dr Philip Nitschke was born in South Australia and did his early educational training in Adelaide, where he graduated with a science honours degree and then did a PhD in physics. He travelled to the Northern Territory in his twenties to become involved in a number of socially relevant issues, where he worked with Aboriginal people in what was the first major land claim in Australia.

Following a serious accident he took the opportunity during a lengthy convalescence to study medicine, graduating from Sydney in 1988. He returned to the territory, working as a medical photographer and a doctor.

Following a protracted whistle-blowing incident at the hospital over radiation issues, he left to work with intravenous drug users. This was when he was 'enveloped' by the euthanasia issue, on which he has been working virtually full time ever since.

Introductory comments

A number of Australian states have spent considerable time debating the issue of euthanasia in recent years. It was the Northern Territory which successfully passed a bill in 1995, thereby becoming the first state in the world to have enacted a euthanasia law.

The Northern Territory is about the size of France and Germany combined, but with a population in the region of 150,000. The bill was enthusiastically promoted by the Parliamentarian Marshall Perron, who, following a number of personal tragedies, decided to introduce a bill to legislate for voluntary euthanasia.

The measure was opposed by the Australian Medical Association, religious groups and Aborigines, but they failed to stop the bill being enacted on 1 July 1996. Dr Philip Nitschke was not only instrumental in supporting Marshall Perron in his campaign, but became the first medical practitioner to end the life of a patient following the new legislation.

The interview with Dr Nitschke explores a number of key points in the euthanasia debate. Dr Nitschke is strongly critical of the principle of double effect, believing it to be hypocrisy on the part of the medical profession. He describes the principle of double effect as 'double effect death'. He believes that it is wrong to send people to a 'pharmacological oblivion' often lasting a number of days. Dr Nitschke believes it is time that the principle of double effect is abandoned and a more honest approach taken to the care of the dying.

A further point which Dr Nitschke emphasises is the role of the medical profession. He shares none of the concerns of some doctors that legalising euthanasia would fundamentally change the role of a doctor from someone who cures or cares to a killer. On the contrary, he believes that the current hypocrisy of medical practice at the end of life does little to instill confidence in the medical profession. Dr Nitschke states there are three groups of practitioners in Australia: those who won't practise euthanasia, those who do but won't admit it, and those who do and would like to see a change of law.

Dr Nitschke is leading the way in developing new

technologies to assist people to die, thereby demedicalising the process. As he outlines in the following interview, Dr Nitschke believes that this will prevent the politicians from considering the matter and will speed up the process allowing voluntary euthanasia. He himself has already developed the laptop machine he calls Deliverance which he explains in detail during the interview. However, looking to the future he and other colleagues are interested in developing euthanasia drinks and pills which people will be able to take themselves, free from any medical intervention. This is a new development in the debate.

Dr Nitschke predicts that shortly after the millennium the Northern Territory's Act will be reinstated following political changes. Making comparisons with the abortion legislation of twenty-five years ago, he describes the push as relentless and the change as inevitable. He concludes that once one state has euthanasia legislation it will be impossible for the other states in Australia to oppose it. Predicting that the courts will play an increasing role in the issue as they refuse to convict people involved in assisting the death of a relative, Dr Nitschke believes that technology will ultimately allow us to practise voluntary euthanasia free from the hands of the medical profession.

Interview

Perhaps we could begin by discussing the recent legislative changes in Australia and in particular the Northern Territory. Press reports in the UK have followed the recent debates in the Northern Territory. What is the current legislative position?

The federal government have recently overturned the new Northern Territory law, so leaving the Northern Territory in the same position now as the other states of Australia. In other words, assisting someone to end their life is illegal.

There are moves in two states to try and introduce pieces of legislation which the federal government would not be able to overturn. The Northern Territory legislation was simply rendered unacceptable while it remains a territory. However, there is a move among people for statehood for the Northern Territory. Should this come about, then the original euthanasia legislation would have to be represented and is likely to pass. The Northern Territory would then become the first place in Australia which actually had a piece of working legislation back on the books. This looks likely as the proposed legislation in Western Australia and in South Australia is meeting all sorts of obstacles within the state parliaments.

Can you explain how the recent Northern Territory Rights of the Terminally Ill Act worked in practice?

The Act enabled a doctor to assist a person to end their life provided a number of requirements were satisfied. The person had to be terminally ill, over the age of eighteen, have had their prognosis and diagnosis checked by another doctor, have received some input from palliative care doctors and have had a review by a psychiatrist to make sure they were not suffering from clinically treatable depression. Provided they continued to request assistance to end their life and providing a cooling-off period had elapsed, then a doctor could administer a lethal injection. The method was not specified.

Did you use the law yourself before it was replaced?

When it was law I was the first person to make use of this legislation and I had worked very hard to get the law into place. We knew for a year beforehand it would become operative on 1 July 1996. The legislation was actually passed on 25 May 1995 so there was quite a period of time before it came into operation. During that time I was being approached by patients who wanted help, but I wasn't able to help them legally until 1 July 1996.

We had an awful lot of trouble getting the law to work. There was a whole range of difficulties with the legislation and it was under attack from all quarters. Challenges came in the courts, and ultimately it was defeated by the successful strategy of overturning it using the political process in the federal government. It was operational from 1 July through to its overturning on Good Friday the following year, 1997, so it was operational for about eight months. In that time I had four patients who successfully used the law. They all had lethal injections from the machine that I had developed, whereby they effectively initiated the process themselves even though that wasn't required in the legislation – I could have just given them a lethal injection. Only four people satisfied the criteria during that time.

The British press had a very interesting article on a lady called Jan Culhain. Perhaps you could state a little more about her case.

Yes. She was one of those people who turned up in Darwin before the legislation was in place. There were about four or five people who came to Darwin who would have satisfied the legal requirement but they were there in that period after it had been passed but before it was actually enacted, so they were not legally allowed to be helped out. Of those people most of them died, usually with assistance in some illegal way. Jan Culhain wasn't a person who had to act very quickly because although she had breast cancer it was in a somewhat quiescent state and so she had quite a bit of time. She arrived in Darwin asking to be helped. She was unable to be helped, so she started to go through the procedures that were needed to demonstrate her eligibility. In a sense she became an example of how the law was working. During this process and the cooling-off period she halfway satisfied her criteria, and then she decided to let things go and she is still living in Darwin. At this stage she doesn't feel she wants to go ahead with it.

The four people who were assisted, what conditions did they have?

The first person was Bob Dent. He was the first person in the world to die making use of voluntary euthanasia legislation and he was suffering from prostate cancer. He was a territorian. The second person was a woman who had come up from South Australia. I mention that because we had a lot of trouble up here when we were trying to get the law to work, with immense difficulties with the hostility of the medical profession in Darwin, who had to be co-operative. One of the things they were complaining about was that some of these patients were coming from inter-state.

The second one was from inter-state, she was a woman called Janet Mills who had an unusual cancer, the same as Paul Eddington, the British actor, a skin condition called mycosis fungoides. The third person's name was never released – he was a local male with stomach cancer – and the last person was a woman from Sydney who came up suffering from breast cancer.

13

The first person ever to turn up came on the first day of enactment, 1 July. He was a taxi driver from Broken Hill who had stomach cancer, and we simply couldn't get the law to work for him. In desperation he drove his taxi back to Broken Hill where he died a week or so later. He was the first person there who saw the law not working. It took another couple of months after that, with an awful lot of work, to try and convince a recalcitrant medical profession to change their views. Some of the publicity over the first person, Max Bell, prompted one or two of the specialists in the Northern Territory to break ranks, and actually helped Bob Dent.

Was there a common factor in the four people which precipitated the request for euthanasia? Perhaps a loss of dignity, acute pain, fear? Were there some common features in each of those four tragic cases?

Yes, there were, and the same factors occur with those who frequently contact me for help. One can see some underlying unifying characteristics in this group, and the one that most comes to mind is that they are people who have always been in control in their lives. They are people who have never easily had others make decisions for them; they tend to be people who run their own lives. They have been confronted with a horrific diagnosis and their approach is to try and do something about it, and normally they have tried everything. Having failed at every other treatment or approach that has been offered, they are not the sort of people who now feel that they want to sit back and let others do their worrying for them; they want to keep an active and assertive role right through to the end. It seems to be a psychological profile that is the unifying characteristic.

Some of them had pain, but pain wasn't the overwhelming

symptom. Mostly it was this feeling in general that the whole package wasn't good enough. This was the case even with the last patient to come up here, who had very good palliative care in Sydney. She didn't have any nausea, vomiting or incontinence, or anything else. However, the palliative care people could not accept her view that she didn't like the fact that this disease had so debilitated her. She couldn't get out of bed and do the things she wanted to do which she had always been able to do up until her seventies. It really was that frustration and not wanting the disability that these serious illnesses were bringing.

In England, people would say the answer to this problem is the hospice movement, advanced palliative care. They might question whether or not Australia has got enough services in that area. How would you react to that sort of argument which is often advocated?

Yes, we hear a lot of it. It was used ad nauseam up here because the Northern Territory is a very small population with limited and sparse services, and it was the original response from those who would overturn the law, which was a very popular law, and still is.

I think the absolute argument against this view was the fact that two of the four people I helped to die, and a number of the others who turned up and were not able to use the law, were coming here even though they had the best palliative care in Australia. I must say that by the end of that period of operation of the law, palliative care services had been expanded remarkably by a government sensitive to this particular criticism. They put a lot of effort into developing palliative care services in the Northern Territory. There was a requirement in the legislation that palliative care advice had to be sought for each of these patients, but people with the best palliative care in Australia were still coming to Darwin to die.

People who argue that good services remove the need for euthanasia know they are lying, and every now and then you'll find palliative care doctors who admit, usually privately, that they simply cannot solve all the problems. There is a small group of people who receive palliative care and do not find the services offered satisfy their needs and requirements, and they still wish to go ahead and die. It is a small group, but everyone wants that right. That is why the legislation was popular, because everyone in Australia, 70 per cent at least, thinks that one should have that right even though only a very small group of the dying will actually act on it.

There has been a discussion that the palliative care movement in the UK can deal with 96 per cent of cases of cancer pain. In the remaining 4 per cent they have difficulty but can achieve it even if at times the patient loses consciousness. Don't you think that's a more appropriate way of terminal management than shortening the patient's life?

One person I have not mentioned was a woman who was unfortunate, for the federal government overturned the law even though she had satisfied all the requirements, a woman called Esther Wilde. She was dying of carcinoid syndrome, a cancer, and had been holding off, waiting for the right time, when the federal government acted. The Senate voted to overturn the law and she lost her chance. A particular amendment had been attempted by one of the supportive Green Senators in Australia to try to allow her to have that option but it was overturned by a Senate vote. She couldn't go ahead because she was so well known and so much publicity had surrounded her plight.

We were forced to go down the path of slow euthanasia,

whereby the patient has an infusion of drugs which effectively keep them in a state of being unaware of their suffering. 'Pharmacological oblivion' is the term that's used, I like the phrase 'slow euthanasia' and I have seen it used quite commonly by palliative care services, in hospices around the world. When the situation becomes too difficult someone will suggest they will run some morphine through an infusion, mixed up with another drug, which tends to take you off the planet and the person lies there peacefully, like a baby.

The people who use these drugs often say that they are not actually shortening the patient's life, they are simply treating the pain and discomfort and rendering them peaceful. We went down that rather macabre process with Esther Wilde. I set up the infusion. I was getting advice from one or two of the palliative care specialists in Australia, who agreed that this is complete hypocrisy because these drugs of course do shorten your life. No one is actually saying the truth. You cannot expect these drugs to run through you and be good for your health. Esther Wilde curled up like a baby and stayed there for four days until she finally died.

I have spoken a lot about the hypocrisy of that sort of approach, and I am the only person in the world who has been able to see the difference between that approach and the procedures that we were allowed under a decent piece of legislation. The essential is that Esther Wilde, a nursing sister, did not want this to happen to her. She made it very clear and knew exactly what I was talking about when I said I could give her some drugs which would make her feel comfortable. She ended up having to say yes, because she had absolutely no choice – she just wanted out.

Very few of that 4 per cent you were referring to are going to say they want to be put into pharmacologic oblivion until then. What they are going to say is, 'I want to die.' You can either listen to them or say, 'I'm not going to do that.' I think to mess around and give them some sort of protracted four-day death is an obscenity. It shows the hypocrisy of the medical profession that they would do that, using drugs that they know are shortening that patient's life, even though they won't say that. That, I think, is a illustration of how corrupt the profession has become on this issue.

I take it from what you have said that you would have little time for the principle of double effect, the legal principle which applies in the UK, allowing doctors to increase the dosage with the foreseen but unintended consequence that it may shorten life?

No. That's exactly the principle we're talking about here and I have got nothing but contempt for those who would further that view. Double effect is complete hypocrisy – the idea that we treat the pain but if the person should accidentally die or we shorten their life, so be it. What we're about is addressing the problem of the patient's pain. Double effect has replaced the words 'slow euthanasia'.

Can we discuss some of the technology that you have been researching and advancing which has been used in assisting patients to die? Can you explain how Deliverance works and how you came up with the idea?

I came up with it because I had little contact with terminally ill patients until I became involved in the political struggle to try and get the legislation through up here. Because of that I got some publicity and then I started to be approached by terminally ill patients a long time before the bill was in position. I was confronted with these problems all the time about whether I would help them or not, and if I did I would have to do it illegally, with all the risks.

One of the themes which came up with terminally ill people was that the law was finally going to be passed and would come into operation some time in the future. People would often say they didn't want to mess around all the time. They were a group of people who were fiercely independent, that was one characteristic I noticed. They would have preferred to be in control even up to the point of administering their own drugs and would have done quite well under the Oregon legislation, whereby all the doctor does is write out a prescription for tablets. The patient goes home and takes them themselves. This is a group who wanted to do that, although they didn't necessarily want the worry and uncertainty which comes from oral medication. They wanted an injection but recognised the fact that they couldn't give it to themselves. I told them it wasn't too difficult to arrange.

We can actually change it from voluntary euthanasia to assisted suicide by the simple provision of a device that will administer the injection. That is where the idea first developed of a simple syringe driver with a button to start it, which is really a development of what Dr Jack Kevorkian was doing in the USA. His idea of using a piece of apparatus that the patient initiated was a very simple and effective device which made it assisted suicide, although people were in no doubt that the patient was initiating the process themselves.

I developed the syringe driver, instead of Kevorkian's scheme of gravity feeding of drugs. The critics started with the idea, 'What happens if there's a mistake and someone accidentally presses a button?' As a way of deflecting the criticism the laptop was adapted. It was just a more complex switch, really, as it would simply ask three statements and you had to respond appropriately by pressing the space bar as opposed to any other key. This was a way of being certain that you were in fact lucid and that you could breathe and act appropriately, so there was no suggestion that you were lying comatose and some unscrupulous relative was coming along and pressing the button so that they could get your inheritance. This was really the idea of the laptop.

Each of those four people who used that laptop computer rushed through those three questions as fast as they could and pressed the space bar on the final one, and fifteen to twenty seconds later the syringe driver started up. In any period in those fifteen to twenty seconds they could have stopped the process by pressing any key, but as it was they all turned away from the computer as soon as they had pressed that last button. Three of them were with loved ones. Fifteen to twenty seconds later the machine started up and the drugs were delivered intravenously. The person was asleep within seconds and had died a few minutes later.

How would you describe the atmosphere in the rooms where there were loved ones present?

I never left any of those rooms feeling that I had done the wrong thing. I came out feeling it was exactly the right thing to have done.

There was immense relief on the part of the people involved when they had finally made use of the law and knew that it was all over. I suppose it was all over once they had got all their signatures in place for using the law and they relaxed at that point. When the final day and the final stage arrived they looked as though they were really welcoming the death that was coming. They were immensely happy that they were now able to go ahead and end their lives, and felt relief on behalf of their loved ones that the suffering had come to an end.

These were experiences I will never forget. They were always extremely difficult experiences for me, and I found them very hard to go through. Nevertheless, having gone through them I found it was exactly the right thing to have done.

You are now developing technology which would take the doctor right out of the situation?

Yes. The legislative approaches are floundering because politicians refuse to bite the bullet on this. It's hard to understand when something is so overwhelmingly popular, and this has been demonstrated every time there's a poll. We know what people think about this issue. Yet that small but extremely well-organised minority manage to make quite sure that no politician really has the guts to tackle this issue, and they have just caved in completely on this. This is partly because this issue doesn't fit neatly into either the left or the right of the political spectrum; it cuts across the spectrum like no other issue, so no political party wants to take it on. Politicians would prefer to let this disappear, as they did, and overturn it rather than listen to the wishes of the electorate.

This has left a huge pool of very annoyed and upset people in Australia and there's a lot of pressure to do something. I'm getting contacted quite regularly by dying people asking and begging me what we're going to do about this situation, so, as one can't wait for the politicians, there are a couple of other approaches.

There's the legal approach, with a series of test cases, similar to the UK. Annie Lindsell and people have moved the issue along through what's happened in the courts. That's certainly an approach which will persist here, too.

I suppose there's a technical solution: that's the idea of the so-called suicide drink or pill, whereby we develop a product a person can get hold of to end their life. It won't be policeable. It will be ubiquitous enough to be obtained for

21

the drink; the ingredients could be manufactured at home by people wanting to go down this path. This sort of technical solution has the ability to totally change the face of this issue and that's where quite a bit of effort is going now. As legislation looks unlikely, a technical solution makes eminent sense.

This suicide drink – I believe you've been disseminating information about this on the Net, is that right?

Only the theory behind it. There's been no information about how you would go ahead. The rationale, or philosophy if you like, was up on our home page as to why we are going that way, really to head off the inevitable criticism. You get criticism from voluntary euthanasia groups as well as from your opponents.

Everyone, apart from all the people who contact me day after day asking for help on this issue, seems to think that such research is something they don't wish to have anything to do with. As I said, it would be nice to have legislation, but we have not got it.

The UK papers have not covered in any detail your own personal motivation in campaigning for a change in law. Could you explain what motivates you with regard to euthanasia? Is it questions of autonomy, quality of life? You must be strongly motivated in order to be so involved in something that's taking up so much of your time and effort and, I imagine, affecting your medical career quite considerably?

Yes, it's brought it to an end in many ways; I simply don't have the time. It's not as though I had this high on my list of social changes I wanted to see. I had not been a member of an association or a society, I'd been involved in a lot of political issues in my life and I did medicine very late in life.

My background is wanting social and political change in various issues, which you would see as libertarian-type issues – questions of race, trying to get more humane treatment for intravenous drug users in the Northern Territory and other issues. When the announcement was made by our leader of the government, who personally drafted the bill, it was really the first I knew of it, certainly the first time I'd ever really thought about voluntary euthanasia.

It became clear after the announcement was made that the medical profession would make sure this law never worked. The thing that goaded me into action was the feeling that the profession itself was behaving in such an arrogant way and expecting to dictate to the community, because it was clear the community at large thought the bill a very good thing. When the Australian Medical Association said they would make sure this law never got off the ground, it was that which drove me. I could not stand that degree of elitism and that degree of arrogance from a small group within society, especially a group of doctors. I thought it was misleading to claim that no doctors would support this law. There were some, not many, so I set about trying to find a group of doctors in the territory who would come out publicly and say the bill was on the right track. I only managed to find about twenty out of five hundred in the territory. Those twenty were able to come out and take out a page advert in the press and destroy the myth that there wasn't a doctor in the territory who would help this law work. We began to have an impact on the community and on the other politicians. We got a group together who thought it was a good idea, and these were names that were printed publicly.

These were the main reasons behind my involvement. I had little to do with dying patients. I had no particularly harrowing experiences with loved ones. I'd seen different cultural attitudes to death and was somewhat cynical to the Western attitude, whereby we compartmentalise our dying and make sure the well in society, especially the young, never see a dying person. That was completely different to what I saw in Aboriginal camps where the dying were involved in the life of the living, which struck me as being far more reasonable.

You are very critical about the AMA and your colleagues in the medical profession. Maybe they are against euthanasia because it's contrary to what they see as the role of a doctor: namely, you are overstepping the mark from where you are caring for someone, if you can't cure their illness, to actually killing them. Maybe some of them have an ethical framework which would not tolerate euthanasia. Are you not being a bit harsh on them?

Maybe they do, and I respect them. Unfortunately the doctors split into three groups. Primarily there are those you just described – they have got more integrity than those who do help people to die but do not want anyone to know about it. This second group are those who have always helped their patients to die but prefer it to remain under the carpet, behind closed doors, to happen illegally. It's very similar to the abortion legislation twenty-five years ago, where certain patients, if they were lucky, had the right contacts and enough money, could always get access to safe abortion. So that group are also getting access to help with euthanasia now.

This group of doctors don't want legislation, they don't want sunlight coming into this particular practice which goes on, and they want the totally unregulated jungle which currently exists. Of course, for the patients who want help, it's completely inequitable. It depends on whether or not you know one of these doctors, and if you have enough money or not. There's a great deal of hypocrisy within the profession.

Then there's the third group of doctors, in which I include myself. We are those who want this process regulated and controlled, made more egalitarian for the people.

Because there is a large group of doctors in the middle who are ambivalent to the whole thing, they would come out publicly and say that they don't want any legislation. They certainly don't want legislation and they work very hard to make sure we don't get a law. If there's a chance of a law they work hard to try and have it overturned. These are the ones I view with contempt. In terms of that group who say it's not part of their ethical belief system and don't want any part of it, there was never any suggestion there would be any compulsion on doctors to assist. The legislation made it very clear that doctors who did not want to have anything to do with it would not need to. It's the fact they were then prepared to shove their views down other people's throats which is what I find so difficult to tolerate about that first group that you referred to.

It's a very helpful distinction between the three groups. The second group is often referred to by the pro-euthanasia supporters in the UK in a similar vein. Surely the burden of proof is against your argument, because if they are practising euthanasia, the death certificate and the drug regime would be quite clear and, as with Dr Nigel Cox of Winchester, they would face a trial? Surely that must be the case in Australia as well?

Those who are assisting now are doing it very privately and it's not surfacing. They are certainly not drawing attention to these particular incidents. These are people who make quite sure their practices and activities never see the legal light of day. A good example of this is in the gay community, with the HIV-supportive doctors who make suicide very easily available and work for people who are part of that network, part of that club. They work with a great deal of secrecy; it's almost impenetrable. I have actually tried to get some assistance from doctors who work in this group, for my own group of patients in those early days, although it's totally different as mine were elderly cancer patients and these were younger HIV patients. Such was the secrecy of the brotherhood, if you like, it was absolutely impenetrable. They argue it has to be like that because of the legal penalty if one's caught, it's so great.

What drugs are they using for this activity?

An assortment of drugs, but they tend to use relatively readily available drugs in intravenous form like morphine and valium or something along those lines.

How can they kill using morphine? If you talk to a hospice doctor, they say it's very difficult to kill someone with morphine.

It is indeed. Just a simple injection of morphine, especially among people who are in hospices, is unlikely to kill. In contrast to those with HIV, those in hospices have cancer and have had lots of exposure to morphine, so they become extremely tolerant to it and you can run grams of morphine intravenously, enough to kill ten people, and it won't even touch them.

However, if you mix it with a barbiturate, it becomes far more lethal, given intravenously. It is simply going down on the death certificate as people dying from HIV. No one is looking into the actual deaths; they are not having autopsies or toxicology, so doctors who are helping can get away with it quite commonly.

Obviously these doctors are providing a service at considerable risk to themselves and quite a deal of anguish. Perhaps I was rather scathing originally – I don't actually mind them helping, what I object to is when they then stand in the way of having a piece of decent legislation put in place.

Doctors in the UK treating someone in a hospital would have a carefully monitored drug regime.

That's true. That's why it's very difficult once a person gets into an institution to do anything other than to provide perhaps a double effect death. So within the hospices themselves, you don't find people coming along and giving you injections of barbiturates to end your life – you simply cannot get away with it. But out in the community you can. The HIV doctors I'm referring to are not talking about death in hospices, or institutions, but death at home. In that situation you can get away with murder, and that's what's going on. No one will ever know about it unless you decide to tell them.

Presumably you are in favour of voluntary euthanasia for anyone whose suffering is unbearable and has made an expressed wish to die?

Yes. 'Expressed wish to die' means they are lucid and confident and have not got identifiable, treatable depression. Unbearable suffering strikes me as being a good criterion as opposed to the one we had in the territory, which was terminal illness and led to all sorts of definition problems. Some of the new pieces of legislation I referred to in South Australia and Western Australia have broadened that out to use the words you just used, 'intolerable suffering'.

You would include in that motor neurone disease, Alzheimer's, psychiatric depression, severe geriatric conditions?

Let's take these one by one because they're all different. Motor neurone disease, I would certainly agree with you. Alzheimer's disease is an impossible situation because they simply cannot give consent. Psychiatric depression would be seen as something treatable. With severe geriatrics, if a person is so old they have decided their situation is unbearable, I suppose they make it into the unbearable suffering class, but it's not a disease as such.

There was an interesting case in Holland, the Chabot case, where a doctor was prosecuted for giving a fatal injection to a patient who was not suffering from a terminal condition. Have you got any views on that one?

This was the case of the woman suffering depression. My understanding was that the psychiatrist involved was certainly seen as someone who acted in a very brave and courageous fashion. The idea of attempting to set up a contract with a patient to try and help them but ultimately to carry out their part of the bargain rather than to try to double-cross the patient, I think shows a great deal of medical integrity which is something we rarely see.

The dilemma is that such a patient would never have been encompassed by our piece of legislation, as they would not have been seen as terminally ill, and they would not have been able to be helped. My own personal views are that this was a very courageous doctor, and I like the idea that some-one tries desperately to engage with and help a patient. It has some similarities with my work with intravenous drug users. Most of my work, other than the euthanasia issue, is with them. I engage in contractual arrangements with people like this all the time. I attempt to go part of their way if they can come a bit my way. We try to work some middle course out. If it can't be done and if the contract breaks down, there's some obligation on me to do what originally I have contracted to do. In the case of intravenous drug users it's often to do with the procurement of narcotics and the like.

Opponents say that voluntary euthanasia is impossible to police, that it inevitably leads to involuntary euthanasia. They quote the Remmelink Report, which gave a picture of euthan-asia in the Netherlands in 1990, when more then three thousand deaths were attributed to the practice. They say it leads to a euthanasia mentality, with people feeling pressuri-sed into asking for it when perhaps they don't want it. Do you accept this?

People do quote the Remmelink Report, and they are very quick to dismiss the follow-up report written five years later in the *New England Journal*. The editorial in the *New England Journal* said it's hard to portray these figures as a descent into depravity. The actual study couldn't really identify any slippery slope. If it brings about a new mentality in the profession, one would say it's about time, because the mentality we've got at present, whereby we will simply deny listening to and acting on the wishes of suffering patients, is a dreadful mentality. If we're going to say that's the way it's always been and that's the way we're going to leave it, we're going to leave 70 per cent of the population totally unhappy with the views of the profession. I have this idea that the profession has to serve the people. It doesn't just sit here and act in a unilateral fashion developing its own standards without any relationship to the society which it purports to serve.

What about people feeling pressurised to ask for euthanasia? It's back to squaring one person's autonomy with another's. Surely everyone's autonomy has to be balanced?

Yes. It's certainly an argument which is discussed a great deal, the belief that one must balance personal autonomy with obligations to society. It's an argument you can develop in a very sophisticated way, and in many ways it seems to be unanswerable. There has to be some balance, and I don't believe we should simply turn our backs on the faces of the suffering and say we can't help you because we fear that this may in some way alter the dynamic within society. I think that sort of harshness, which I see, and I saw it especially in the case of Esther Wilde when the Australian Senate voted, is not the sort of society I want to see.

There's a price to pay in society for disallowing euthanasia. In fact, that particular price doesn't lead to an enhancement in our society at all. So if we are going to look at the group effects or societal effects of euthanasia, I would argue that what we have at present is damaging to society. We can improve that by listening to this very vulnerable group within society and not turning our backs on them.

You say that the majority of people in Australia are in favour. Is that an NOP poll?

Various polls have been undertaken. The Morgan polls have been run since 1946, asking the same questions since those post-war days. The question was straightforward, asking: if you were terminally ill with no hope of recovery, would you think a doctor should be able to help end your life? The rate responding positively started at 46 per cent just after the war and it's been rising ever since. In the last fifteen years it's been in the mid 70 per cent with that particular question.

There were many other polls with a question asking people for their views on the territory law. It always came out the same. Excluding the religious groups, the only group that came out with less than 50 per cent support for that question were the doctors. Nurses didn't think like that and no other identifiable group thought like that, and the community average was 77 per cent.

Do you think that popular opinion should dictate the ethics of the medical profession? In Britain the vast majority are in favour of the death penalty. I can think of three immediate reasons why it would be wrong to legalise the death penalty in this country and think that those in favour are misguided.

At some point you have to decide whether you are going to live in a democracy or not. The fact that you expressed such disquiet about the ability of the masses to make decisions which will ultimately benefit society is a worry to me. In some ways, what you are advocating is being ruled by an elite, and I'm not at all happy or comfortable with that. I certainly get asked this question about the death penalty a lot and I feel the same disquiet.

Ultimately I see democracy as being very fundamental and important. My job is to make sure people don't want the death penalty. While I think we can do that, I don't think I can convince people they don't want voluntary euthanasia. I just can't do that. I think we can run a very winnable campaign to make sure that we do not vote in favour of the death

31

penalty. I don't think they, the elite, can run a campaign to get the people to say they do not want the right of assistance to end their lives.

I talk quite commonly about the role of elites within society, and in this case it's the medical elite who see themselves as being the ones who know what's best for society. Those sorts of attitudes underpin the difficulty the profession seems to have in coming to grips with the fact it does not have the God-given right to make rules for society.

Some people who are against euthanasia in the UK see it as a religious debate, a debate about the sanctity of life. Do you see it as a medical issue, with perhaps a traditional view to healthcare practice? Do you believe life is sacred or sanctified or valued?

I agree that the opposition is the Church. We've had this battle here and I think we can win against the profession but we didn't win against the Church. The Church is the force making the politicians crumble. They ran campaigns which were very effective given the fact they have a small group of people in society who believed in what they were doing. I don't want to underrate the role of the Church, but I get called upon more to comment on the profession and the role the profession took in the actual political process which led to the overturning of our law.

In terms of sanctity of life, these are views I can certainly acknowledge, but if you don't subscribe to that belief system, what do you do then? I find it offensive that a small group who believe in the sanctity of life in some ways force the rest of us to comply with their belief structure.

Where do you think the debate is going to go in Australia now?

I was talking to Marshall Perron recently, who was the politician who introduced the law although he's no longer the leader of the government in the territory. Along with statehood, which allows the federal government to overturn territories' laws, the law will come back into place. It's likely by 2001, with statehood, that the territory itself will be the first place in Australia to have a piece of functioning euthanasia legislation. It will be the same law that I have already made use of.

The other two pieces of legislation are having a very difficult time in South Australia and Western Australia, although that's not to say they won't survive. South Australian legislation has passed the first vote in the Upper House. That's the first time that's ever happened in the state. There are similarities with the abortion legislation battles twenty-five years ago. The whole process of getting legislation through is one step forward and two steps back, and you mess around for a decade trying to get these things through. The push is relentless, though, and I see it as an inevitability. We will get this change, it's just a question of where and when. Everyone's watching closely to see what happens in Oregon, of course. The pressure is starting to mount. If we had kept our legislation in place for much longer it would have been impossible for the other states in Australia not to introduce such legislation. They couldn't have their citizens moving across state boundaries to try and access a piece of civilising legislation in the North. For the very fundamental reason that politicians seem unable to address this issue, it's going to take a very long time and in that period we will see the various test cases in the courts. We will see juries refusing to convict people who are involved.

I get involved in the illegal deaths of quite a number of

people these days and sooner or later I might find myself in a courtroom. I don't have dreadful fears about this because I feel very secure in the fact that juries themselves would be very unlikely to convict me if I were to be put on trial.

The final issue is the one I have talked about, which is the development of a technical solution. It's part of a strategy to put pressure on the legislators to move, but it's not just hypothetical. We are working on this in a very serious way, too. It could work in the same way as the development of the abortion pill, which will change the whole face of abortion – a technical solution which takes it out of the hands of the doctors and demedicalises the issue. I think there are many reasons to try to demedicalise the questions of voluntary euthanasia.

Dr Andrew Fergusson

Biographical details

Dr Andrew Fergusson qualified in medicine from St Thomas's Hospital, London, in 1979. His medical experience includes four years working in hospital medicine followed by ten years as a general practitioner in London.

Since 1989 he has worked for the Christian Medical Fellowship in the UK, a membership organisation of over four thousand doctors. His role has involved lecturing, writing and broadcasting on ethics.

In 1991 he became Chairman of HOPE, Healthcare Opposed to Euthanasia, a forum for healthcare professionals who are against euthanasia. He has played a significant role in debating the issue of euthanasia in the UK media.

Dr Fergusson was called to give evidence to the House of Lords Medical Ethics Committee and has contributed to many other reports and papers on euthanasia and related issues.

Introductory comments

As mentioned on a number of occasions in this book, the question of definition does not go away. Dr Fergusson states clearly that for him euthanasia, namely the killing of a patient as part of their medical treatment, is defined by the intention of the doctor. A doctor failing to take a course of action which is appropriate medical treatment could be as guilty of euthanasia as a doctor who intentionally shortens the life of a patient by injecting them with a drug such as potassium chloride. While Dr Fergusson is not suggesting that every possible treatment should be used in all circumstances, he believes that an omission can intentionally bring about the death of a patient.

It is not surprising, therefore, that Dr Fergusson views the Bland judgment as a landmark case in British law. On this point he shares the concerns of Melanie Phillips and Lord Walton of Detchant. However, he brings to his defence Professor Singer, a well-known spokesman in favour of euthanasia, who described the Bland judgment as a land-mark case leading to a ground-breaking change in the Western world's understanding of the obligations of medical ethics.

Dr Fergusson believes that the principle of double effect is an adequate framework, and the best devised to date for dealing with the difficult decisions at the end of life. It provides an effective way of defining what is appropriate and acceptable treatment and enables doctors to act in an ethical framework but without the fear of prosecution. Dr Fergusson believes that the problem with the principle of double effect arises from those who do not understand some of the basics of medical ethics. The patient's life may indeed be shortened, but this is unintended. The intention all along is to relieve the suffering of the patient and to use the latest palliative techniques in achieving that goal.

Rather than ditching the principle of double effect, Dr Fergusson believes that more open discussion regarding drug regimes and palliative techniques would prevent any con-fusion emerging and that new pharmacological guidelines would assist doctors to understand a little more of the impact that drug regimes will have upon their patients.

Dr Fergusson states that there is common ground between those who are against euthanasia and those who are in favour of a change of law. He states that both groups would like to see more open discussion about death and dying, which remains a taboo in our society. Following recent advances in medical science, it is often the individual who has a quick death who is envied rather than those who have a long and drawn-out degenerative condition. In times past a slower death was seen as an opportunity to put matters in order; now, however, many people fear that high-tech medical treatment will be used at the end of their lives, postponing their death. Dr Fergusson recognises that the advances made by the palliative care movement in considering the holistic care necessary for dying patients have done much to break the current taboo surrounding death and dying.

Interview

How would HOPE define the word 'euthanasia'? There seems to be considerable confusion over the use of the word which is witnessed in the debate. I wonder if you might be able to state clearly how those who are opposed to euthanasia define it?

The word 'euthanasia' comes literally from two Greek words, *eu* and *thanatos*, meaning 'well death' or, more poetically, 'gentle and pleasant death'. It's the sort of death we would want for ourselves and our loved ones and our patients. The expression has traditionally meant mercy killing, but in the international debate at the moment there is confusion about the definition. In my own view, that confusion is brought about deliberately by the pro-euthanasia lobby, often in order to get headlines and appear to have more people supporting their cause than really do.

After a long series of discussions in the early 1990s the founders of HOPE agreed on a definition which has become widely accepted in the euthanasia debate: that euthanasia is the intentional killing by act or omission of a person whose life is felt not to be worth living. The key concept in that is the word 'intentional', a reminder that lives can be ended intentionally by not doing things just as they can be ended intentionally by positive acts – a lethal injection, etc. We would modify the definition 'voluntary or involuntary, non-voluntary' as needed later.

The definition is very helpful but it does not solve all the confusion. Not all people would accept that omitting treatment is euthanasia. On the contrary, they might say it is good medical practice.

The key concept with regard to euthanasia is that of intention. Nobody in HOPE argues that doctors or other health professionals are under an obligation to give every possible treatment to every possible patient in every possible situation just because those treatments exist. It can be perfectly good medical practice to withhold a medical treatment altogether if, for example, the burden of it were to outweigh the benefit of it. The key concept is the intention of the omission, and if the intention of stopping a burdensome treatment is to give the maximum possible quality of life to a dying person in the increasingly precious time that remains, that is ethical. If the intention of omission is wholly to bring about their death, then I would argue that that's unethical and it's euthanasia.

Where does HOPE stand on the withdrawing of nutrition and hydration from patients in persistent vegetative state? It seems that the issue is concentrated on how you view the provision of food and water. Can it be withdrawn or is that euthanasia?

Persistent vegetative state is thankfully a rare condition and it's one where I think we can safely say that hard cases make bad law. Normally the provision of nutrition and hydration would be standard basic care performed by nurses, other health professionals or by family and voluntary carers. It would be standard care to give all living human beings food and fluids simply as a reflection of the care they deserve because they are living human beings.

The time when food and water can be withdrawn is when people are at the very end of their lives. Nobody would think it appropriate or just or kind to force food and fluids down somebody in the last few hours of their life, although one would want to pay attention to comfort and oral hygiene and so on.

A helpful question to ask is: 'Is the patient I'm looking after in the process of living still, or are they in the process of dying?' If they are genuinely close to the end of the dying process, then food and fluid may become much less of a priority. The difficulty with PVS is that, philosophically, that question, 'Is this patient in the process of living or dying?' arguably doesn't apply, and so I think PVS is very much a one-off situation.

My own opinion is that while I can entirely understand the arguments of all involved on both sides of the debate, in my own opinion the British courts' decision with the late Anthony Bland did in fact for the first time legalise intentional killing by omission, however that was worded. I think that represents a fundamental shift of British law. That's not just my opinion. Professor Peter Singer, for example, a leading advocate of the worldwide pro-euthanasia cause, would look to that verdict as an absolute landmark, a ground-breaking change in the Western world's understanding of obligations in medical ethics. What interests me is that in the five years or so now since Anthony Bland died, out of several thousand patients in the UK who have gone into PVS and come out of it naturally – by which I mean they have died a natural death – only about ten cases have come before the British courts where health professionals and families have asked for withdrawal of food and fluid.

Perhaps this is suggesting that in maybe 99 per cent of PVS cases the intuitions of the family and professional carers are that it is right to carry on with food and fluid, and their intuition is that to withdraw it would be an intentional killing by omission. So the law has done one thing, but I don't accept that people's consciences, people's intuitions, the ordinary feelings of most people involved in these situations, have changed.

What do you say when faced with an individual who's had a relative die in pain, or when you are faced with the argument that we put our animals down, we would put a dog down, but we have to watch our loved ones and relatives suffer? Are you not flying in the face of common sense?

I think as long as people are dying badly we will have to debate euthanasia. The House of Lords Select Committee recommended, when it reported early in 1994, that if we are going to say no to euthanasia we have to say yes to the best possible palliative care. It's ironic that this debate rages when in fact we now have the ability, through the pioneering work of Cicely Saunders and others, to look after dying people better than ever before. Hospices are welcomed, they are popular. Palliative medicine is a concept, it's not bricks and mortar, it's a way health professionals think about the appropriate goals of care. Everybody, including the pro-euthanasia lobby, agrees that palliative care is an excellent thing, and the debate then is whether or not voluntary euthanasia is ever a legitimate option within palliative care.

In short, my first answer is that people do not need to die badly: we can do better. The whole compassion case for euthanasia stands or falls on the concept of *force majeure*. Do we have to kill the patient in order to kill the symptoms? My other point, coming back to the animals issue, is that human beings are not merely animals. An animal is unable to find any sense out of the experience of suffering at all. I believe that suffering is always a bad thing and that doctors, health professionals and others should do everything legitimately possible to reduce the amount of human suffering, but I think my general practitioner experience was that patients were not surprised by the news that they had a terminal illness. Hurt, frightened, angry that it had happened now, etc., but fundamentally not surprised. We know it's the lot of all humans that we are going to die, and I think I can honestly say that, in fourteen years of clinical medicine, I was never involved in the difficult cases of suffering and dying people without, sooner or later, both those people themselves and their loved ones finding something good in this somewhere. I'm not saying that suffering is a good thing, it's a bad thing and we should do everything legitimately possible to reduce it and eliminate it, but I think at the end of the day we have to accept that the human condition means there is going to be some suffering. One of the things that being human means is that I look for what this experience can teach me and can teach my loved ones, and can teach the human community.

Surely hospice care is only part of the answer? It doesn't deal with the problems of severe geriatric decline or with Alzheimer's, motor neurone disease or other degenerative conditions that we are now experiencing as a result of the advance in medical science. Hospice care only affects a small number; it cannot be the answer to euthanasia if there are many that it cannot help.

First, some hospices at least are moving into degenerative neurological disease, like motor neurone disease, and some hospices are admitting patients who have advanced cardiac failure or advanced respiratory disease. But I did say earlier that a hospice is not about bricks and mortar. Palliative medicine is a principle, it's an approach to medicine, it's an approach that recognises that we are all going to die one day and therefore asks more fundamental questions: what are our real goals now?

I think the euthanasia debate is driven by the fact that death is currently a taboo in our society. There are all sorts of philosophical and general cultural and religious reasons for that, but let me just talk about medical science. We have had such wonderful advances this century that we get the impression that medicine can cure anything. Doctors like curing, health professionals like curing, and we struggle to cope with the right way of handling situations when we can no longer cure. Some doctors will even say, 'There's nothing I can do for you.' That's always wrong: there may be nothing more I can do to cure you but there is always something more I can do caring for you and being with you. I think that's the key lesson that's come out of the palliative medicine movement. So, when we come on to chronic degenerative disease, which two-thirds of us are going to suffer, I think we need to recognise that we are all going to die one day. How am I going to prepare for that?

Our predecessors wanted to have the benefits of a long

drawn-out terminal illness so they could put their affairs in order and prepare to meet their Maker. Nowadays it's the guy who drops dead suddenly who's envied, he's the lucky guy. I think that different approach to the nature of dying and death shows us the problem that we have. I would suggest, therefore, that we don't need to spend such huge sums of money and effort on inappropriate, invasive, painful, unpleasant, burdensome high-tech care at the very end of life. We have a dialogue with the patient, we get the issues out in the open, we talk with them and their families about what's really important now. By all means offer the surgery, the chemotherapy, if it's appropriate, but if it is not then we concentrate on caring which goes beyond trying to cure. The real answer to that question is that the whole of society needs to think about death and dying, and what, if anything, happens after it, and it needs to prepare for death in a better way. I think the money that's liberated from the inappropriate use of high-tech medicine could be put towards the personnel costs, because palliative care really is cheap in everything except people's time. It could be put towards the personnel costs of looking after people more.

You are not being fatalistic?

I'm not being fatalistic, I'm not being nihilistic, I'm very grateful for the wonderful advances in healthcare. It's just that I think we have lost the art of medicine just as we have gained in the science of it. So I think the key answer to this is a complete reorientation of the way we as a whole society look at medicine, and I'm convinced voluntary euthanasia is not any part of the answer.

The pro-euthanasia lobby would share your sentiments re-garding opening up a debate on death. They would take it further and ask, 'Why can't you stage your own death?' Why can't you think ahead and decide, if you are facing a degener-ative condition, that you wish to create a time where, with your loved ones, you have a doctor assist you to die? You don't have to waste thousands of pounds on nursing care in an unhappy state, knowing it might be more happily spent on grandchildren. You want to face death; why not be able to manage it?

I acknowledge that our opponents in the euthanasia debate would agree with much of what I have just said and I would go as far as to say we substantially agree about the diagnosis of the direction in which healthcare should be reorientated, but we disagree about the treatment. They will say it is sometimes right in controlled circumstances for patients to make decisions about their own death – physician-assisted suicide, voluntary euthanasia. Our side is saying that is never right. We are moving from here, perhaps out of the realms of healthcare into the realms of philosophy and law.

Speaking as a Christian, yes, the issue does begin with the sixth commandment, God saying, 'Thou shalt not kill,' but I have had to ask myself the tough question: 'Why does God say that when I have faced patients in very tough situations which we have not been able to relieve entirely?' I have had at least one patient repeatedly ask me for voluntary euthanasia. I have had to face illness in my own family and the answer, which I think is applicable to people of different religious faiths and none, is all to do with the concept of justice, of treating like alike.

In short, to change the law to allow voluntary euthanasia would be moving from the current position, where we have got an absolute black and white situation in UK law, that the lives of all legally innocent citizens are of equal value and are given equal and total protection from being taken. We would be moving out of that absolute prohibition of intentional killing to a shades of grey situation. Could we find effective guidelines to control the shades of grey? I think the Dutch evidence, not least, shows us very clearly that it is not possible. Even in a legally controlled voluntary euthanasia scenario, what happens is that a doctor makes a quality-of-life decision about a patient.

Now, the voluntary euthanasia lobby will say nonsense, it's the patient who makes the quality-of-life decision and the patient is best qualified to judge. I would reply, yes, quality of life is important, patients are the best judges of it, but in a legally controlled voluntary euthanasia situation the doctor has to agree with the patient's quality-of-life decision. In other words, in law it's actually the doctor who's taking the binding decision. I could suggest scenarios when of course it would be quite inappropriate for doctors to make such a quality-of-life decision, and we know that even in Holland doctors don't agree in more than 50 per cent of euthanasia requests. What we are suggesting is that we move from a situation where every UK citizen's life is equally protected to one where doctors are allowed to make quality-of-life decisions. Doctors are human, they will get some of those decisions wrong for a whole range of reasons. The people in the voluntary euthanasia lobby who talk about the integrity and the character of British doctors – well, I can only conclude that they have just not come across some of my colleagues. We are all human; doctors are no different.

The concept is one which we have looked at very seriously in Britain in the very major House of Lords Review in 1993/94, and we concluded against euthanasia. The majority of doctors don't want it and I believe that society does not want it.

On that point, what are the statistics for doctors not wanting it? What evidence are you using for that?

I think with statistics, surveys, opinion polls, it's very easy to quote those that back you up. I think there is a difference between some recent polls published in the general practitioner newspapers in Britain and the recent vote at the BMA's annual representative meeting. At that meeting doctors knew weeks in advance this item was on the agenda; it would have been discussed in their local divisions and they would have turned up mandated to vote on serious ethical matters. In the major debates in 1992/93 in Torquay and again in Edinburgh in 1997, the official voice of the deliberated BMA opinion was overwhelmingly against on both occasions.

But in answer to that, the pro-euthanasia lobby would say that doctors in the UK are practising it every day of the week, you should go and talk to them. They are scared of admitting it, but that's what they are doing. What would you say in answer to that?

I think there is a lot of confusion, coming back to the definition of the word 'euthanasia', about what is going on. Doctors do, when appropriate, use larger doses of opiates, morphine, which may possibly, on very rare occasions, shorten patients' lives. Those occasions are very rare. Even in the perhaps one in a thousand or so where that is true, if morphine is used properly the intention of the doctor in using that large dose of morphine is the perfectly proper one of controlling a patient's pain and distress. There's no other way of doing it, and not to do it would leave the patient in unrelieved pain and distress.

There is a deliberate manipulation of this issue of intention, and the phrase 'the doctrine of double effect' may be unhelpful. Double effect could be taken to mean double standards, hypocrisy. The issue medically and philosophically and legally is perfectly clear, but many qualified doctors in Britain are open to being persuaded that they are practising euthanasia already, when in fact they are acting with the intention of relieving pain.

Second, the number of doctors actually doing it is small. I sit in a position where I hear stories, I have people ring in, nurses in hospital teams saying, 'I'm worried that doctors are doing this, that or the other to a patient who is also under my care.' We talk about the details and very often there is misunderstanding about the impact of the drugs. I do not accept there are large numbers of British doctors performing lethal injection euthanasia or lethal omission euthanasia. If the pro-euthanasia lobby think there are, they should put up, and if not they should shut up.

The principle of double effect sounds confusing. Can you explain from your own medical experience how it works in practice? There is a need to assess whether it is hypocrisy, with doctors practising euthanasia but not admitting it, or whether actually it is an ethical and adequate framework for caring for people who are in pain.

First, the drugs in question are all related to morphine. They are called opiates as a class of drugs, and the common ones used are morphine and diamorphine. They are incredibly useful drugs with a whole range of life-saving attributes. In medical practice I carried diamorphine for injection in my GP emergency bag, and I saved the lives of people who had just had a heart attack or heart failure with it. They are also very useful for relieving pain and a range of different distressing symptoms that people who are dying might expect to experience. Breathlessness and anxiety would be two further symptoms. One of the things that the hospice movement has taught us, thanks to Cicely Saunders' research and the research of others, is that it is perfectly safe and appropriate to use doses of those drugs which hitherto would have been thought ridiculous or intentionally lethal, provided a doctor will work a patient up to those big doses slowly. If you used a significant dose of morphine for the first time in a patient who had never had it before, you could quite easily stop their breathing and they would die if you didn't use the antidote and reverse it. But if you built up to that big dose of morphine gradually over weeks and months, because that was the dose of morphine that patient needed for those symptoms to be controlled, then not only do they not die, you don't shorten their life at all. They actually will live a longer life with a higher quality of life.

I can remember, for example, looking after a woman in general practice dying at home over about a year with widespread cancer, and we worked up in terms of her needed pain relief to about 1,000 milligrams of oral morphine a day in several divided doses, together with other things. I would visit her two or three times a week; I'd get there mid-morning and she would just have completed the *Daily Telegraph* crossword when I got there. She was on a dose of morphine which in black and white, in print, must be lethal, but we learn that it is not. I have heard an expert in palliative medicine, one of the leading consultants at St Christopher's, say that in his experience using those sorts of large doses of morphine shortens life in less than one in a thousand cases. But let's assume it's one in a hundred, or even five in a hundred cases: we need to come back to the question of intention. The patient is in pain, they are agitated, they are anxious, they are distressed; perhaps they are distressed by breathlessness as well. Those are all unpleasant things. Human charity requires that we do what we can to help them, and if that patient gets great relief from large doses of morphine and he is one of the one in a thousand or one in a hundred or five in a hundred for whom life is perhaps shortened, then we say to ourselves, 'What was the intention?' The intention was the perfectly proper one of getting on top of his symptoms when nothing else could do it, and not to treat him thus would be a neglect of duty. As a foreseen but not intended side-effect of that dose of morphine, his life was shortened.

Ethics and UK law allow this because of the perfectly proper primary intention of relieving distress. Now there is a potential weakness in this position, and that's how do we know what the doctor's intention was? That intention may not be perfect, but, a little bit like parliamentary democracy, it's the best thing we have come up with yet for these sorts of end-of-life medical decisions. I would propose two safeguards. One is that decisions like a big increase in the dose of opiates should be taken out in the open; they should be discussed if possible with the patient, with the patient's family, with all the people on the healthcare team, with everybody who's got a legitimate interest to know. I think some of the high-profile euthanasia cases we have heard in Britain this decade have been doctors who have cracked under pressure when they were on their own. Palliative care is a team approach, so decisions should be taken out in the open in a dialogue with the patient, who is an expert in two things at least – how he feels and what he wants.

The second safeguard I would argue for in this question of intention is one of pharmacological guidelines. The drugs in question are called controlled drugs in law; there are strict rules on registering the amounts that are used, by whom and when – there are checks on that, and if the hospital pharmacist came back on duty on Monday morning and discovered that five kilograms of diamorphine had been used on a single patient over the weekend then he would rightly ask questions and institute an investigation.

Intention may not be perfect but I think, philosophically, ethically, legally, it's the best we have got and in practice it can be safeguarded.

On the principle of double effect, it seems to me an important point is the actual effect of an increased dose of diamorphine or morphine on an individual. If the drug cannot kill, then the doctor's intention cannot be to kill. In your medical experience, is it easy to shorten a life with diamorphine? Is it easy to predict what will happen when diamorphine is increased? How does that compare to using a drug like potassium chloride?

When you are using opiate drugs like diamorphine in a patient for the first time, you have no idea what the effect on that particular patient will be. There are some medical conditions, chronic respiratory disease for example, where you need to be particularly cautious. You know that in all patients with chronic respiratory disease, but in general you don't know: you start off with a small dose and you keep increasing it until you get to the right dose. That's the lesson of the palliative care movement and, as I said earlier, we therefore sometimes need to use very large doses. But in people who have been on diamorphine for a while it is actually very difficult to kill them with diamorphine.

If I can come, with some reluctance perhaps, to the case of the late Mrs Lilian Boyes, the patient whose life Dr Nigel Cox ended in the summer of 1991, coming to court in 1992, he actually gave her, I think, 100 milligrams of diamorphine intravenously, and it had no effect on her whatsoever. There may have been some very technical pharmacological physiological explanations for that, but the point I wanted to make was that it didn't kill her. It's actually very difficult to kill people with diamorphine. Dr Cox, I think, cracked under the pressure of the moment, but, I am prepared to accept, with the best of motives. He meant well; he thought there was no other way to help this patient. Then he used a different drug altogether, he used intravenous potassium chloride in a one-off dose, what we call a bolus, and that drug in that situation could have no intention other than to stop Mrs Boyes' heart. It's the drug used in heart surgery at the moment when the patient's heart and lungs have been by-passed and we want to stop the heart in order to start operating inside it. You use a slug of potassium chloride intravenously and the heart stops.

That's what Dr Cox did with Mrs Boyes, and her heart stopped. His intention was to end her life by stopping her heart and he succeeded. It was not difficult to kill Mrs Boyes with potassium chloride in that way, whereas it is difficult to kill people with diamorphine. We are back again to that concept I have stressed throughout this interview, the concept of intention.

One of the issues I wanted to raise with you is the whole issue of personal autonomy. It seems to me that you've advocated hospice care in that it has developed staggering new initiatives in the field of pain relief. You've advocated the importance of intention both to the law and to medical practice, and how a breach of that would be a very dangerous road to go down. A lot of people say that it is my right to die; why can't I exercise my right, why can't I write an advance directive to tell you in advance what I would or would not like? Are you rejecting the principle of personal autonomy and thereby being symptomatic of the established section of the medical profession, rather than the new doctors who are just coming out of medical school and are willing to accept the autonomy of the patient?

I think this is a very good question. I certainly qualified in

1975 at the very end of the era, the high point of the era of doctor paternalism when Doctor gave Doctor's Orders and Doctor was always right. It was a nonsense, and broadly I welcome the cultural swing that there's been altogether over the past twenty years, and particularly in healthcare, towards a recognition of patient autonomy, self-determination, 'whose life is it anyway?'

I think the problem we have got now, not just in the euthanasia debate but in many areas of healthcare ethics, is that the pendulum has swung too far and the patient is calling too many shots. Healthcare should be a partnership of experts: the doctor, the nurse, the healthcare professional, who are all experts in their own speciality, and the patient, who is an expert in two things, how he feels and what he wants. Big healthcare decisions should be taken by a dialogue, a partnership of two equals. That means that both sides of that partnership have rights and responsibilities. The patient certainly does have rights to patient autonomy but they are not unlimited rights. The patient actually has responsibilities. The doctor does have responsibility to the patient but the doctor also has some rights, and most doctors feel they have a right not to be pressured to kill their patients. They feel that's outside thousands of years of medical tradition and is the start of getting on to a very slippery slope.

Returning to the question of patient autonomy, it's a nonsense to think that in any area of everyday life we have complete autonomy. We obey speed limits, we stop at red lights, we drive on the left-hand side of the road, and so on. Why? Because of our own safety but also for the safety of other people. It's John Donne, 'no man is an island', or the biblical quote that no man lives to himself alone and no man dies to himself alone. However much we might want it, we cannot be completely isolated in contemporary society. Whether we like it or not we are in a relationship with other people and that gives us responsibilities. So the law reflects that responsibility and the whole argument about autonomy in the euthanasia debate can be expressed in a secular, utilitarian way.

Many people who ask for euthanasia don't actually want it. Let me justify that comment. Doctors in general and palliative care specialists in particular know that behind a request for euthanasia is really a cry for something else – take my pain away, will somebody please tell my wife so we can talk about this, will somebody please tell me what's going on, I'm afraid of dying like this or this. Behind the request for euthanasia is nearly always something else, and I believe that in the vast majority, well over 90 per cent of requests for euthanasia, the patient really wants 'something else'. I do accept, though, that there is a small minority of fully deliberated requests – I won't call them rational for technical philosophical reasons, but they are fully deliberated requests – and again there is a point of agreement with the Voluntary Euthanasia Society that such do exist.

The question is, why can't that small number of people for whom the request is fully deliberated be allowed their 'right' to have their life ended by a doctor (because the expression 'right to die' is of course asking for a right to be killed by a doctor, let's not mince words there)? The answer is, to change the law to allow that small minority their 'right' we would be putting at risk the safety of a much larger majority, for whom euthanasia would not be the right thing to do, so that small minority suffers for the sake of a much larger majority. That may be a secular utilitarian argument but it's a powerful pragmatic argument about why we should not change the law. The law of civilised Western societies puts an incredibly high value on the life of each human individual for very good reasons. There are different religious or philosophical explanations for that, but we tamper with it at our peril. In short, patient autonomy is not absolute.

Why can't you maintain your personal ethical position not practising euthanasia and accept the development of clinics where perhaps you create a new practitioner, a cross between a doctor and an anaesthetist, a new person, Kevorkian style, who is willing to undertake euthanasia for those who don't wish to go to a hospice, don't wish to go to hospital and have made a rational decision because of unbearable suffering, whatever it may be, that they want to die?

The question is talking about the place of conscience, and of course in all their proposed legislations the voluntary euthanasia movements say, 'Of course we won't pressurise the Dr Fergussons of this world to do it,' etc., and your suggestion that we create a new medical speciality, perhaps called 'thanatology' or whatever, is to me a distasteful and a repugnant one.

Leaving that conscience clause debate aside, I think it's entirely a secondary one and I don't want to begin to discuss it because we are not going to change the law to allow euthanasia. I think what we have to bear very strongly in mind is that when a society, a state, changes its law, three things happen. The first one is obviously that we do whatever the new law has said, but the second thing that happens is that we go further than the new law has said. As evidence for that I would briefly cite the UK experience of thirty years of the Abortion Act, but in the euthanasia debate I would cite the Dutch euthanasia scenario, where one in three euthanasia deaths in Holland in 1990 was not voluntary. The majority of euthanasia deaths are still not reported to the appropriate Dutch officials so we have no way of checking whether guidelines are followed. There's plenty of evidence in Holland today for a slippery slope on euthanasia.

The third and most important thing that happens when we change the law is that we send a signal to society. We change the very moral climate of opinion within which individuals take decisions. As a GP I counselled on average one woman a month requesting abortion, and often that woman's argument was that the law allows this so it must be OK and it must be OK for me. Therefore, to change British law further to allow the intentional killing of adults, young people, children, babies with serious illness, would send an incredibly strong signal to society that would actually change the moral climate of opinion within which healthcare professionals and patients took their decisions. The option to choose voluntary euthanasia might become for some altruistic grandmother an obligation to choose euthanasia, so she's got more of a nest egg to leave the grandchildren.

I understand your logic, but what if someone feels that terminal decline through a degenerative condition is so undignified they would like to receive assistance to a dignified death? You know how to help them – should doctors have the courage to do it?

I think the overall question about dignity is getting back to the fundamentals of what it means to be a human being. I think the present drive for dignity is really saying, 'I don't want to be dependent upon anybody else,' and I think that is secular humanistic autonomy taken to an impossible extreme. It's people saying, 'I am an island; I want to remain an island,' and I'm afraid the bottom line is, John Donne again, no man, no woman is an island. We are interdependent, we are in a relationship with each other whether we like it or not. I think, therefore, sometimes we have to accept care from others. It doesn't reduce our dignity if we do so; in fact I would suggest it increases it, it positively enhances it, providing that care is given in a proper and a loving way. I don't think we are born with, or we acquire by the age of twenty-one, say, a hundred units of dignity and every illness and every loss reduces from that. I think dignity in a sense is a bit like beauty in the eye of the beholder, and it's up to carers and all of us in society to add to people's dignity by the way in which we treat them and help them to come to terms with progressive losses. So I think the whole 'death with dignity' debate needs a much more open discussion and to get back to its fundamentals.

I'd like to finish by looking at the whole international debate, because there seem to be activities going on in other parts of the world that have a great deal of relevance to what's happening in the UK. Opinion polls suggest that many people's gut reaction is in favour of euthanasia. Opinion polls in the United States have been in favour, there have been changes of law in Australia, which were later overturned, and the Dutch have created a unique legal framework to accommodate it. Do you see an inevitability about what is happening internationally which will impact the debate in the United Kingdom and result in a change in law?

I have been the Chairman of HOPE, Healthcare Opposed to Euthanasia, for seven years now and I'm very interested in the way I believe the debate within the UK has altered. When I started broadcasting seven years ago, I was always viewed with scepticism. The media, by their nature, are liberal and always anxious for change – I was a reactionary, paternalistic old fuddy duddy, a religious fundamentalist, etc. But over the years, and the last two or three years in particular, I have sensed a shift in approach. I sense that the media are keen to hear both sides of the debate. I think that reflects the fact that we have had more time to think about this.

There are certainly arguments for legalising voluntary euthanasia and they are often made well, and need to be refuted. Superficially the compassionate, humane thing to do does seem to be to say yes. Somebody stopped briefly in a shopping mall on a Saturday morning may well say yes, depending on how the question is worded. This interview has lasted for nearly an hour; it's taken me some time to start making at least some points, and I think it is clear that, when the opportunity for those points to be made and to be heard is taken, thoughtful people will conclude that there is more to this than meets the eye.

You could argue the jury is still out on this one but I'm confident that we will not lose this, either in this country or elsewhere in the world. The Australian legislation in the Northern Territory was shortlived and has been overturned. The Supreme Court of the USA in spring 1997 was unanimous, saying that US citizens had no constitutional right to physician-assisted suicide. That did put the onus back on individual states and we know what Oregon has done, but people were surprised that the most rights-driven society in the world accepted the arguments I have been making in this interview. The Dutch medical profession is strongly criticised within Europe, most of all by its European neighbours, the Germans. Germany is now the most conservative country in Europe on medical ethics. On almost any subject, you ask them why and they give you a very short answer: 'Because of recent history.' In fact, I think the debate among the professionals is on level terms still and, if anything, is moving our way, and I could cite two further recent indications in the British Parliament to back that up.

The debate among the population at the grass roots is in danger of being won by feelings, by images from biased reporting, by intentional engineered confusion or by wishy-washy woolly-minded thinking on this issue. Therefore, I think it's essential that we define terms, talk about all the possibilities and get real. Above all, it's essential that if we are going to say no to euthanasia, as I believe we will, we say yes to good palliative care, yes to a national debate about dying and death, yes to what are our priorities in healthcare spending. We get it out in the open, we talk about it and we are prepared to put our money where our mouth is.

Returning to international developments, I understand by 2010 there will be 200 million people in China over the age of sixty-five. Obviously we know the statistics for Western Europe and the expected demographic changes. Won't the pressure for euthanasia be driven by the pressure on state healthcare budgets for overseeing the vast numbers of people who are suffering degenerative conditions?

I think this so-called demographic time bomb argument is an important and significant one, but I don't think in the middle of 1998 we can predict where China will be in 2010. I don't think any futurologist would dare to stick his neck out two years, never mind twelve. I think the world population situation in many healthcare ethics debates is largely a red herring, and I say that because if we provide proper education, proper social service provision, proper healthcare, then people will choose, for example, voluntarily to limit family size. That's what we've seen in the Western world this century. I don't want to get sidetracked into the whole abortion/contraception debate. That does still leave us, of course, with large proportions of elderly people. I think the answers are that we need to recognise that three score and ten is all I have, four score if I am strong. We know that roughly half of all healthcare spending in the developed world takes place in the last six months of an individual's life. Well, surprise, surprise! People die of illnesses and illnesses need treatment and treatments cost money, but even so we could be much more appropriate in the way that we think about spending, and that's a very broad-based discussion. Therefore, what I do think we need worldwide is to bust the dying taboo and to talk about this, to get real and to make choices. I think it's possible that in an entirely altruistic and non-coerced way some elderly people might think about their obligations to the other citizens on the planet when they are considering whether to go for a third operation in the course of this particular cancer, but I would want there to be no coercion possible. People of all persuasions would agree that it's wrong to coerce on the grounds of sex or age or race or whatever. We need to care for each other equally; we are all equal citizens in one ever-shrinking world community, even if the number of members of that community is at present continuing to grow. There's an old saying, 'If you take care of the pennies, the pounds will take care of themselves.' I think if we take care of individual life and death and decisions I would be confident that we would all still be here in 2030.

Dr Jim Howe

Biographical details

Dr Howe is a graduate of Queen's University, Belfast, and works as Consultant Neurologist at Airedale General Hospital. He trained and qualified as a geriatrician. As well as doing neurology work, Dr Howe has also looked after a younger disabled unit, so has experience in rehabilitation medicine.

Dr Howe was Tony Bland's doctor. In his first major interview since the case he talks openly about Tony Bland and the decision to withdraw his feeding. He has frequently given evidence in cases before the High Court and regularly lectures on the subject to students of law and medicine.

Introductory comments

The case of Tony Bland still causes considerable controversy among healthcare professionals. Among the general public, there was considerable confusion at the time of the case, with a number of papers wrongly referring to Tony Bland being on a life-support machine.

The case reveals a significant number of disagreements among the healthcare professionals. Some referred to the food and fluid which Mr Bland was receiving as artificial, a form of medical treatment which could be of no further benefit to him. Other healthcare professionals would draw back from ever referring to nutrition and hydration as artificial, seeing it as the means of sustenance. Some recognise the case as a sensible judgment in the light of the individual's circumstances, while one doctor predicted it would lead to 'the cleansing of long-stay wards'.

Some have suggested that the case should never have been brought, that antibiotics should have been withheld at an earlier stage and therefore the request for the withdrawal of nutrition and hydration would not have been necessary. Others, culminating in Cardinal Winning in an interview in this book, have suggested that the case was a conspiracy, an attempt to change the law with regard to euthanasia, to legalise the intentional killing of a patient, with the Bland judgment being the case that breached the dam.

The House of Lords Select Committee on Medical Ethics, when considering this case, stated that the progressive development and ultimate acceptance of the notion that some treatment is inappropriate should make it unnecessary to consider the withdrawal of nutrition and hydration. The Lords Select Committee was divided on the issue of the Bland judgment but was able to agree on this specific point. The significance of the case was not lost on the Law Lords who considered it.

When the local authority, with the support of the Bland family, sought and received a declaration from the High Court which was later confirmed by the Court of Appeal, the House of Lords had to consider the matter in the light of its significance. Two of the Lords of Appeal called for Parliament to consider the matters, they deemed them so significant. Lord Brown Wilkinson said it was 'imperative that the moral, social and legal issues raised by this case should be considered by Parliament. If Parliament fails to act then judge-made law will of necessity, through a gradual and uncertain process, provide a legal answer to each new question as it arises. But in my judgment that is not the best way to proceed.'

While the case raised the issue of whether it is ethically acceptable to withdraw nutrition and hydration, it also raises poignant questions about the condition of persistent vegetative state. A certain degree of controversy remains about the definition. Some practitioners will not accept that it is possible to be sure of the cerebral activity within patients who are perceived to be in a persistent vegetative state. Could the patient be in a deep coma, where the loss of consciousness may be temporary, or in the so-called locked-in syndrome, where the patient is conscious but disabled, so that communication is only possible through blinking or voluntary eye movements? Concern has been expressed about regular misdiagnosis. Dr Keith Andrews of the National Centre for Neurodisability in Putney has shown clearly that some patients admitted to hospital in what was originally regarded as a vegetative state have demonstrated substantial recovery, with the return of useful function after several months or even longer.

Dr Jim Howe was responsible for the care of Tony Bland following the tragedy at Hillsborough. Here, Dr Howe discusses in detail the background to the decision to withdraw nutrition and hydration. He describes some of the tests and repeated clinical observations undertaken on Tony Bland, and answers some of the critics. He goes on to reveal his support for voluntary euthanasia under certain circumstances, and outlines his view that killing can be a caring thing to do if the individual legitimately, freely and automonously decides they do not wish their life to continue.

In justifying the outcome of the case Dr Howe expresses his belief that Tony Bland was no longer a person. His personhood had gone following the accident.

Interview

The House of Lords Select Committee on Medical Ethics spent considerable time debating the Bland judgment. You mention that you thought the Committee report was deeply flawed; to which recommendation were you referring?

I question the conclusion that if you don't give someone in PVS antibiotics they will die and you don't have to withdraw feeding. That's just nonsense. Human beings have survived without antibiotics for thousands and thousands of years, and plenty of patients who are severely disabled or are in a vegetative state don't get antibiotics and live on for year after year.

The specific case they were referring to was Tony Bland. In that case, was there an aggressive regime of treating with antibiotics?

No.

So he had not survived lots of infections?

He had survived repeated infections without antibiotics. We treated his chest infections and urinary infections.

One of the suggestions of the House of Lords Medical Ethics report was that, as it becomes more acceptable to withdraw treatment at an earlier stage, then questions of withdrawing nutrition and hydration will be unnecessary.

That is just not right, because if you do not give patients

antibiotics they will survive infections. Even quite frail elderly people can survive infections without antibiotics. It is a myth to think that they will die. I think this line was taken so that they could produce a unanimous report, as some members of the Committee were strongly against withdrawal of fluids. Since the Committee I have spoken to Lord Walton and Baroness Warnock, and she agreed with me that it was wrong.

Surely Lord Walton, with all his experience in neurology, must know that patients can survive without antibiotics, and therefore the question over the withdrawal of nutrition and hydration will increase and not solely apply to Bland?

I think it's a pressing issue for elderly people who are very severely damaged by a stroke or by Alzheimer's disease. People with Alzheimer's disease reach a point where they can barely swallow. In this country, my experience has been that few or no doctors would consider tube-feeding someone who was in a terminal stage of Alzheimer's disease. They just go on letting the nurses get as much food and fluid into them as they can, spooning a bit of porridge in, spooning a bit of tea in, and gradually the patients just fade away and die.

The same thing applies to very elderly people who have had severe strokes. We know they are in great risk of having another stroke, or having a heart attack. They are not technically in a vegetative state but they are as near to it as you could ever see. Are we going to start tube-feeding those patients? Most geriatricians that I know would not. They would not tube-feed someone who was very severely damaged by multiple strokes, and the very elderly.

Dr Jim Howe

What does that person die of when they die?

They will die of chest infections, or they will die of kidney failure through not getting enough fluid.

So most people suffering from Alzheimer's, severe degenerative conditions and those arising out of old age and frailty, are they dying out of a lack of food and fluid?

They are, partly. Someone with Alzheimer's disease who cannot swallow is not getting enough food and fluid, and for someone who has reached a stage of Alzheimer's disease where they are not able to swallow, most geriatricians in this country would not tube-feed them. Most of those I know would not.

We will return to the issue of food and fluid, but I wondered if you could give some background detail to the Bland case. There was vast media attention, some of it inaccurate, on the Bland case as it proceeded through the courts. Many people felt deeply for Mr and Mrs Bland and their predicament. When did you begin to treat Tony Bland, and what happened to him at Hillsborough?

About a month after the Hillsborough football tragedy I was telephoned by a friend who is a neurologist in Sheffield to say that this lad came from Keighley and he knew that we were the nearest hospital: would we like to take him back to Airedale so he could be near his family? As soon as his condition was stable he came back to Airedale.

He suffered a crushed chest with bilateral tension, pneumothorax (air between the chest wall and the lungs, causing progressive collapse of the lungs). According to the evidence which one of the casualty officers gave at the inquest, he was resuscitated at the Northern General Hospital, when he was brought there by ambulance, put on a ventilator and taken to the intensive care unit, and within a couple of days it was clear that he was in a fully developed vegetative state. They took him off the ventilator and he breathed spontaneously; they moved him to an ordinary ward and transferred him to us at Airedale. So he was already showing signs of a vegetative state when they took him off the ventilator in Sheffield.

When he came into your care, what did you give him in the way of tests?

What we began to do was to make sure that he had adequate nutrition and fluid. He had a tube-feed. We took his tracheo-stomy tube out when we were sure that he was able to maintain a clear airway, and he started having physiotherapy to try and maintain flexibility of his joints and get him sitting up.

The nurses treated him as if he was conscious. We got him out in a chair, we took him out of his room into the main ward, we tried all ways we could to stimulate him. He went in our therapy pool in the physio department because we were hoping that there would be some improvement in his level of awareness, but we never saw any.

What indicators were there revealing his level of awareness? Did he make noises, did his eyes open and close?

He would have periods with his eyes open and periods with his eyes closed. He would make groaning and grunting noises, he would cough and splutter if you tried to get him to swallow things. He started if there was a loud noise, he grimaced in response to peripheral painful stimuli, but at no time did we ever see him make eye contact or get him to respond by blinking or by moving anything in response to questions or commands.

Neither the nursing staff, nor me, nor the consultant who looks after our younger disabled unit, who came to see him regularly, nor his family, nor the occupational therapist, nor the speech therapist, none of us were ever able to establish any communication.

Throughout this period his family acted with the utmost dignity. His dad used to come and help the physiotherapist take him into the therapy pool and so on. They visited him every single day until I persuaded them they ought to have a rota so different members of the family came on different days, just to give some of them a break. His sister came regularly, her husband came, uncles and aunts too. We got to know them very well; they still pop in and visit us.

Throughout this time on a daily basis we tried to make eye contact, to see if he could communicate in any way. You just keep trying and trying. By six months there was no sign of communication and there was no sign of improvement, and at that stage I talked to his family about the possibility of withdrawing treatment because I knew that it was legally possible in America and I assumed it would be legally possible in Britain.

The family were in favour of withdrawing treatment and so was I and the nursing staff. In my ignorance I didn't know that it was illegal in the UK, so I phoned the coroner to ask him what would happen at the inquest if we withdrew treatment. He advised me that if I did withdraw treatment and Tony died, I would be facing a charge of murder, because it had never been tested in the United Kingdom. Although it was legal to withdraw treatment from PVS patients in Canada and the USA, it was not in the United Kingdom.

After that advice from the coroner, you then had to decide whether or not to go to court. The relatives decided that they wanted to test it?

At first Mr and Mrs Bland did not want the Trust to go to court. They couldn't see why we should have to, and they didn't want to have to tolerate all the publicity. They were going through a very bad patch because there was all the investigation of the tragedy and who was to blame, and all this pernicious reporting in the newspapers about how it was all the fans' fault because they were drunk. In fact, Lord Justice Taylor reported that the disaster was not the fault of the fans.

The boy had a number of complications: he developed a fistula because of his bladder catheter which needed surgery. A fistula is an abnormal passage from the bladder to the skin, so urine was draining outside but not through the catheter, and there was local infection there. One of our surgeons had to do a minor operation to drain the fluid and the pus. It was at that point that Mr and Mrs Bland decided they would go through with it and they would agree to us going to court. Remember, it was the Trust which went to court and sought the guidance, not the family. Everybody keeps making this mistake. Mr and Mrs Bland supported Airedale NHS Trust's application to withdraw treatment; they did not make the application.

So Tony Bland was receiving medical treatment regularly merely to keep him in his current condition. How was he fed during his time in your care?

Through a naso-gastric tube. We didn't put a gastrostomy into him because it was clear that there was no improvement and none of us thought there was going to be an improvement. Gastrostomies have complications, they get infected, you can get peritonitis; they are just a little easier to manage, that's all, but we had few problems with the naso-gastric tube.

When the food and fluid was withdrawn, how long did it take before he died?

Nine days.

A number of individuals who gave evidence before the House of Lords Select Committee stated that certain members of the nursing staff were distressed by the withdrawal of nutrition and hydration. Was this the case?

Absolutely not true. There was a lot of rubbish written about it by the nursing hierarchy, the Royal College of Nursing and so on. The nurses who were caring for Tony Bland were day in and day out caring for patients who were dying from other things, heart failure and cancers, so looking after dying patients was nothing new to them. They were 100 per cent in support of the family and the Trust in wanting treatment to be withdrawn. Of course they were sad that such a nice young fellow should die, and of course they were sad for the boy's family, but they didn't find his death any different from any of the other deaths that happened on that ward every day – apart from the publicity, of course.

Another suggestion that was made in parts of the press was that these decisions might have been taken for financial reasons. Was that the case?

I don't know what the financial reasons could have been in Tony Bland's case. There were none.

Well, it was costing a lot of money to keep him at the hospital, which would have been paid for out of the annual budget. One article in the press said that it was driven by financial considerations, that, in the end, decisions regarding those in PVS are financial. You would not agree with that at all?

That's a different matter. That's an ethical matter about justice and the allocation of scarce resources. In the case of Tony Bland, it was not driven by financial considerations. However, in a sense it was, because if you are following ethical principles then you must consider the justice argument as well as arguments from autonomy, beneficence and non-maleficence. Every penny that is spent on keeping someone alive who cannot benefit is a penny that is not being spent on someone who could benefit. Someone in persistent vegetative state who has gone through a period of rehabilitation and a period of observation so that you are sure, as sure as we can be, that they cannot benefit from treatment, that is then a waste of money, it is a waste of resource.

Let me give you another example. In our health district I am not permitted to prescribe certain drugs to people with Alzheimer's disease because the health authority consider there is not enough benefit for the costs involved. This drug improves your memory for about six months, perhaps a year, but the disease continues to deteriorate. A decision has been made that the drug is not a big enough health gain to justify the expense. In the same way, there is no health gain in keeping someone alive in a vegetative state, and that is very expensive. Approximately £200–£300 per day is the cost of keeping someone in a bed in a district general hospital before you even add on tubes and food, drugs, etc. So all the time that he was in that bed, not improving, not getting any benefit from the treatment we were giving him, someone else couldn't be in that bed, somebody who might have benefited, with a heart attack or stroke, who could have been rehabilitated and got back home again. That's the argument about justice in the allocation of resources.

Did you ever think about transferring him to the National Centre for Neurodisability in Putney, which is pioneering much of the activity for those in a persistent vegetative state? Would there have been any benefit in sending him there?

It was quite clear that there was no awareness, no improvement, and I don't think they were doing anything we could not do at Airedale. So what good would it have done? Also, the health authority would have had to pay for it. Somebody has to pay. Where do you think their funds come from at the National Centre for Neurodisability? It's outside the NHS, it's not for profit, but somebody has to pay. That's one of the problems about the UK and the way we talk about private and public medicine. We should talk about profit and not for profit. The Royal Hospital and Home is outside the NHS and is run not for profit. The NHS is run not for profit, BUPA is run for profit.

A key factor in the decision to withdraw nutrition and hydration must be the diagnosis. How were you sure that Tony Bland was in a vegetative state with no powers of perception, from which there was no conceivable chance of recovery?

Most authorities think a year of careful observation and a year of attempted rehabilitation is quite enough in PVS. There have been claims made that some patients have regained awareness after a year in PVS. There are very few of these patients. Some of them are people who are late discoveries that they are aware. If people had paid better attention they would have seen that they were aware before the year was up. There may have been a very small number of patients who have regained awareness outside a year, but none of them recovered to anything better than a severely disabled state. People would say that's terrible and point to the chance of making a mistake, but I'm afraid we take much bigger chances of making a mistake every single day when we do operations. We know that for every thousand people we treat we will save so many lives but we will also cause a few deaths, but people are prepared to accept that, prepared to accept a risk and a benefit. So I don't see a problem about giving up on people in PVS after a year. The biggest collection of cases was in the US PVS task force, and they have collected hundreds of cases and shown that the chance of someone regaining consciousness after a year in PVS is very small, less than 0.1 per cent.

What are the medical criteria you have to fulfil to be sure a patient is in PVS?

The criteria stipulate that persistent observation shows no sign of awareness or voluntary communication. That there is no evidence that they can see or follow moving objects. That there should be no swallowing. That they should be incontinent, bladder and bowel. The observation of many different things over a long period of time satisfy you that someone is in PVS.

Was Bland the worst case of PVS witnessed in the UK?

They are all terrible. There are some people who are in what's been called a minimally aware state, people who can only barely communicate a yes and a no to very simple questions, who occasionally appear to look at you and for a lot of the time don't. These are usually people who have had traumatic brain injury. Sometimes it can be very difficult to distinguish between that and fully developed PVS. Some say it's worse than PVS because it must be terrible to have some degree of awareness and complete helplessness.

Perhaps we could focus at this point on the condition known as locked-in syndrome, which is similar to PVS. What exactly is this condition? A recent Panorama programme focused on patients with locked-in syndrome and showed that patients can communicate by blinking.

Yes, people who are locked in can communicate by blinking. It's usually quite easy to see: they can blink their eyes once for yes and twice for no, they are awake, they are alert and they are able to move their eyes in response to questions and commands. That's why, when you go and see someone who you think might be locked in or in PVS or in coma, you ask them to open their eyes if their eyes are closed and vice versa. Day in and day out with someone in PVS, they don't do it in response to command.

Could it be that their hearing has gone?

No. They jump when a loud noise goes off, so you know that sound is hitting the eardrum and that messages are going from the eardrum along the acoustic nerve to their brain stem and stimulating a startle reflex. So the thing that's gone is the interpretation of hearing in the cerebral cortex. The cortex is the part of our brain which thinks and feels and remembers and makes us the person we are. It is the cortex which is destroyed in persistent vegetative state, but the brain stem is still alive. In locked-in syndrome, the cortex is alive and working but there has been damage in the brain stem which stops the brain controlling and moving the limbs and also stops sensations coming in from the limbs to the brain. Vision and hearing are usually intact, and the person can see and hear and respond in locked-in syndrome.

ECG measures activity in the brain. Did Bland register a flat ECG?

Yes, whenever we recorded it.

One of the things said about Bland's brain was that it was in a vacuous state. What happened to it?

If you suffer a stroke, a blood vessel is blocked and a pyramidal-shaped piece of brain dies. It's replaced by fluid because scavenger cells come in and they eat away the dead cells, and eventually there's a cavity there. In vegetative state due to anoxic brain damage, the cells in the cortex of the brain are destroyed. Through lack of oxygen they are dead; scavenging cells come along and eat away the dead material and there's nothing there. So if you look at brain weight, the weight of the brain of someone who's been three years in a PVS is less than the weight of the brain of someone dying from Alzheimer's disease. The brain just shrivels up, disappears, it's gone, and you can't grow new brain cells. That's how we know people in vegetative state are not going to recover. The idea that if you keep them alive some wonderful medical advance will come along and new cells will grow is science fiction.

How do you account for these people who were in PVS, who Dr Keith Andrews has referred to on a number of occasions, who make a recovery? In one case a woman recovered five years after apparently entering PVS.

Some of them are not being recognised soon enough as being conscious to some degree, and if you look carefully almost all of them are traumatic cases, not anoxic damage cases – they have had closed head injury, so bits of cortex have been destroyed and also the connections between the cortex and the body, and different parts of the cortex have been damaged by acceleration and deceleration injury, when the brain swirls about. Those patients can make some degree of recovery, but almost always to a severely disabled state.

Some people would say that it's worse to be conscious and completely helpless than to be conscious and severely brain damaged. If you are only able to answer yes and no to the very simplest of questions, you are not able to take any pleasure in any activities, not able to speak or swallow, what kind of an existence is that? Remember, these patients who recover consciousness from being in a vegetative state do not recover to normality, they recover to a state of disablement. They are severely impaired. If you ask them, they may tell you that they want to be kept alive like that, if you can believe that they are competent to tell you these things. I, for myself, would not want to be kept alive like that.

You would support voluntary euthanasia and a change in law?

I would support voluntary euthanasia, and a change in law with safeguards. The problems I see with voluntary assisted suicide are problems of side-effects for society. For instance, I can imagine if we had voluntary assisted suicide, a patient of mine with motor neurone disease might decide that he wanted to die next week, not next year when he's completely helpless. That would seem to me to be perfectly reasonable and I would make sure he was not suffering from a depressive illness that could be treated.

I could imagine an elderly woman of eighty who might say, 'Oh, I'm tired of all this and I'm just a burden to everybody, so I will opt out now in order to save society from having to pay my pension and send me a home help, etc.' That would seem to me the wrong reason. That shows that as a society we are not treating old people properly, not according them the respect and care that they deserve. So I think if we could devise proper safeguards I would be in favour of legalising voluntary assisted suicide.

Would doctors undertake the practice of euthanasia?

Why not?

Surely patients would not feel quite so secure in the presence of a physician if they are legally permitted to both treat and kill? Won't the elderly feel pressurised to accept euthanasia and spend their savings on their grandchildren rather than on nursing fees?

That's another side-effect which you would have to guard against. You would have to be certain that another doctor would have to certify that it was OK to go ahead, one not connected with treating you. I can also imagine the situation where I would much rather be looked after by a doctor who I knew would help me to die than by a doctor who would keep me alive at all costs.

That's exactly what I meant about safeguards against side-effects. However, if an elderly person wants to give all their savings to their grandchildren and decides they want to end their life to do that, what's wrong with that? If it's their conscious decision, if they are exercising their personal autonomy in this matter, it's no different to an elderly person giving up their organs to their grandchildren, is it?

One of the arguments put forward by people in the hospice movement is that if one legalised euthanasia the advances that have been made in palliative care might be jeopardised and the incentives for future developments lost.

I don't agree with that. I don't see why it should because my experience shows me that most people do not want voluntary assisted suicide. By not legalising it we are preventing a very small minority of people who legitimately want it from getting it, for fear of harming the large majority of people who don't want it and who would never ask for it.

People want good palliative care and lots of people want to stay alive until the very last moment. That's their choice, and we should fund palliative care and fund research into palliative care to do that.

There are a few people, and the best example I have are

those with motor neurone disease, who are not in pain, who are not suffering, who have not got the ravages of vomiting or whatever from cancer, who have decided that they do not want the indignity of total helplessness; they would prefer to die rather than to be in the undignified state of being completely helpless. That's what I feel about myself, so if I have got the skills and the knowledge to kill myself efficiently why shouldn't I offer that skill to someone who legitimately and freely and autonomously decides that they don't want their life to go on? For me, killing that person would be a caring thing to do.

One of the arguments against is the experience of the Netherlands, or indeed the experience from the abortion law in this country. When you get an issue as contentious as this is – and if the Voluntary Euthanasia Society surveys are wrong it might only be a small minority of people who want it – it changes the climate.

I appreciate that – that is what I mean about side-effects – but legalising abortion has not meant that abortion is now free and on demand. I don't see anything wrong with that. As far as I am concerned, the world is grossly over-populated. I would much rather people practised sensible contraception than had abortions, but I personally don't see anything wrong with abortions because I don't believe that a foetus is a person.

What about Tony Bland, did you see him as a person?

No, his personhood had gone when his chest was crushed; he was not a person in the sense that I understand it, in an ethical sense. A person is someone who has the capacity to value their life: that's the definition given by Professor Harris from Manchester, and I think it's the best one I have seen. A person is that creature, that sentient creature, which has the capacity to value its own life, so by that definition chimpanzees and gorillas are persons; we should not kill them, any more than we should kill other human beings who don't want to be killed.

Does a young baby have value as a person?

A newborn baby probably doesn't.

So you do not believe it has any rights?

I don't like the language of rights. I would give it the benefit of the doubt, but if a newborn baby was very severely handicapped and in pain I would not see it as wrong to let it die.

There's no difference if it's handicapped or in pain or if it's perfectly fit, is there? Its value comes from its humanity.

It's not just the value of its humanity. You should not inflict pain on a sentient creature who will suffer. I would not inflict pain on my pet cat but I don't think it's a person, I don't think it has the capacity to value its own life.

You felt, in your own ethical framework, there was no problem with Tony Bland because he was not a person in your definition of personhood, hence the High Court action. The judges decided that Tony Bland needed no further treatment because it would be of no further benefit to him.

The judges agreed that, looking at his best interests, we could not benefit him by keeping him alive, so there was no duty on me as his doctor to continue to keep him alive. It would not be unlawful for me to withdraw treatment.

How could it be in someone's best interest to die?

The judges did not say it would be in his best interests to die, they said he no longer had any interests of any kind, so his interests were not being served by keeping him alive. The argument, which Lord Lester put to the court but didn't get reported, was that Tony Bland had a posthumous interest in how his family would remember him, as a happy, healthy young man who went off to a football match, or as a twisted body in a bed with a tube in his nose, etc.

Is not this so subjective? The older you get the more vulnerable you become. You become more susceptible to feelings of worthlessness, and it would be so morbid if you spent the last thirty years of your life thinking about when you were going to die.

In some ways I think Lord Lester's point is a reasonable argument, and it was brought home to me by something Mr Bland said when the boy was near death. We said that we would leave the tube in case it was necessary to give him anti-convulsants or anti-spastic drugs if there was any worsening of spasticity or any fits occurred, but we didn't have to give him anything like that at all.

One evening, I was helping one of the staff nurses settle him down for the night and she said, 'We have not put anything down these tubes for four or five days now, why don't we just take them out?' I agreed with her, so we took out his feeding tube and catheter and all the apparatus from the room, and it was like a bedroom, with all the flowers and cards. We put the sheets up to his chin and Mr and Mrs Bland, who had been staying in the hospital, came in and said, 'That is the first time he's looked like our Tony since the day he set off for the football match.'

I think people do have a posthumous interest in how their relatives see them. That was the first time Tony Bland had looked to his father like his own son. That's how he looked until he died, eyes closed, peaceful, quiet.

Is not dignity often to do with how we choose to view and treat a person rather than how they view themselves? Dame Cicely Saunders would say you can be incompetent and incontinent, but you can still have an element of dignity.

Absolutely true, and I would like to think we treated him with the utmost dignity throughout the three years he was with us. But despite that, when we took the apparatus away, he looked different. Mr Bland's was a spontaneous remark and it made me cry.

Leading on from PVS, in your mind should not the withdrawal of nutrition and hydration be available for other conditions?

It comes back to someone with Alzheimer's disease. We would not start tube-feeding them. That's the difference. Someone with Alzheimer's disease is going to die in a short time no matter how well you look after them. With the minimum of care you can keep someone alive in a vegetative state for thirty-six years – that is the longest recorded survival. That's what makes it different for me. Or take another example, withdrawing chemotherapy for cancer so that someone slips from a curative phase to a palliative phase in their care: we do that all the time. When it's clear that the chemotherapy is not working any more we settle for all-out palliative care. You do your best for that person, being guided by what they want every single day.

You don't envisage the practice being extended to other areas of medical practice?

It's already happening. If I have got someone of ninety who's had a second or third stroke I would not start tube-feeding. They are dying from medical complications rather than lack of food and water.

One US doctor has stated that it won't be long before our society realises that there is no difference between starving patients to death and injecting them with a poison.

It's not starving them to death. That's sloganising. We are not starving people to death; it took Bobby Sands more than sixty days to die. Someone in a vegetative state is not suffering.

There's no sentient being there. But there is no difference in consequence of withdrawing treatment and injecting a lethal drug.

Do you think in the long term relatives of those in PVS will say it's much more humane to give the patient potassium chloride rather than waiting nine days for the withdrawal of food and water to take effect?

Why, indeed, I have no idea. Keith Andrews has said he would be prepared to give an injection rather than withdraw food and water and I think I would too, if it was legal. If someone wanted to do it at a certain time and date, what's wrong with that? The seven to ten days it takes for someone in PVS to die is no different from the two weeks to three months it takes someone in a hospice to die. There's little difference between those things. A few days gives everyone a chance to get used to the idea and to be at the bedside; it's the traditional way of looking after people who are dying. The difference is that someone in a vegetative state experiences nothing.

Do you think there will come a day when you can inject with a poison patients who are in PVS?

Perhaps. I would not see it as something that would disturb me for patients with PVS, and if it was legal and families wanted it to be done I think I could do it. But I don't see any need to do it as I don't see the period of seven to ten days as ghastly or horrible, because the victim doesn't suffer anything and it gives the family a chance to say goodbye.

During those seven to ten days, what do you do with the patient?

You keep them clean, you turn them, you give them clean sheets and pillows, you wash out their mouth and put artificial saliva in their mouth, artificial tears in their eyes and keep their eyes clean. You don't need to give them any painkillers at all. You may want to give them an anti-spastic drug and you can do that by suppository, or an anti-epilepsy drug for seizures by suppository. But that's all you need to do. Any reaction would be caused by the spinal cord or the brain stem, it's a nervous reaction.

The problem is, it all boils down to what you view as human life. Other people I interviewed agreed in the sanctity and sacredness of life. That seems to be the dividing line: there are two conflicting world views and there is no correlation between them.

One of the things that irritates me about people who believe in the sanctity of life is that they don't extend that sanctity of life to higher primates and dolphins and so on – or maybe they do – because I think they should. They think that we have a God-given sanctity of life. Well, I don't believe in God so I don't see any divine imprint.

The problem with your definition is that 'personhood' is very subjective.

The concept enables us to examine problems with due regard to the consequences. Of course, we must take responsibility for the consequences of our decisions. Professor Harris of Manchester University has articulated concerns over the government's euthanasia programme. People are allowed to die, though their lives could be prolonged by medical technology, because the NHS does not have the resources to treat them. For example, we have a limited number of dialysis machines per head of the population. We as tax payers do not get the opportunity of having a debate between Trident and dialysis machines.

Melanie Phillips

Biographical details

Melanie Phillips is one of Britain's best-known columnists, currently writing for the *Sunday Times* where she writes about social affairs and political culture. She wrote for the *Observer* from 1993 to 1998 following a sixteen-year career at the *Guardian*, where she rose to the position of News Editor. Her columns have earned her a reputation as a fearless commentator of some of the most controversial and ethical issues of the time. In 1996 she was awarded the Orwell Prize for journalism.

In addition to her work as a columnist she has written a number of books and papers. She is the author of *Divided House*, a study of women at Westminster, and co-author with Dr John Dawson of *Doctors' Dilemmas*, a primer on medical ethics. She has also written a recent best-seller called *All Must Have Prizes*, a highly controversial analysis of the current education scene.

Introductory comments

As a leading columnist currently writing for the *Sunday Times*, Melanie Phillips has written regularly on the subject of euthanasia. Her articles have often focused on two specific points, namely the importance to society of the prohibition of intentional killing and the current campaigning activities of the pro-euthanasia lobby.

For Melanie Phillips it is the intention of a doctor which distinguishes between the killing of a patient and the appropriate withdrawal of medical treatment. Many would agree that there comes a point when the duty to try to save a patient's life is exhausted, and further medical intervention may well be inappropriate. In a competent person such a decision can be made following detailed discussion with the patient and members of the healthcare team. This course of action is undertaken because the burdens of further medical treatment will far outweigh any benefits it might produce.

Such decisions can be more difficult where the patient is incompetent. Here a decision would involve making an assessment of the quality of life of another individual, and such decisions can be controversial.

This practice is not euthanasia. There is a clear distinction between withdrawing medical treatment which would be of no further benefit and taking action with the specific intention of shortening life. The difference between the two surrounds the intention of the healthcare practitioner where treatment is withdrawn. Is it done because to continue would be a burden to the patient, or is the intention to kill the patient? The former course of action is good medical practice; the latter is euthanasia. In the interview Ms Phillips outlines how society's prohibition of intentional killing is the cornerstone of law and social relationships; to remove it would have a long-standing impact on society.

In the following interview, Melanie Phillips outlines her criticism of the stance taken by the Law Lords in the Bland case. She believes that the Bland judgment was legalised euthanasia, for Tony Bland was not dying and the doctor was requesting to take a course of action which would have the intention of shortening the patient's life. Comments from

Lord Mustill during the judgment made it clear that the Law Lords were aware of this yet gave a judgment in favour of withdrawing food and fluid. They justified their position on the grounds that the provision of food and fluid via a naso-gastric tube or gastrostomy is a form of medical treatment, and can therefore be withdrawn if it is deemed of no benefit to the patient. Thereby, under current procedures its withdrawal was permitted. Ms Phillips argues against this on two accounts. Primarily she argues that Tony Bland was not dying; he was not suffering from a terminal disease and could have continued to live for another twenty years. Therefore, in his case, it was not withholding treatment which would make a patient comfortable but might lose them a few days at the end of their life.

The second distinction Ms Phillips touches on is that the provision of food and fluid, through whatever means, should be seen as a basic human right. It would be wrong to withdraw food and fluid from a patient, and particularly an incompetent patient who has no way of communicating their concerns on the matter.

Having argued these points in her columns and more recently in this interview, Ms Phillips attacks the 'seismic mistake' which the judges have made in the Bland judgment. She offers a number of factors for their mistake, including the position that food and water is part of basic care which should be provided to all humanity. By defining it as part of medical treatment, the Law Lords were able to grant permission to withdraw food and fluid. Ms Phillips calls for a law to overturn the development of case law as set by Bland as the only way of repairing the breaches that have been made and for preventing further acceptance of euthanasia.

The second major theme of Melanie Phillips' writings and broadcasting on the issue of euthanasia has been the approach of the pro-euthanasia lobby in attempting to change the law. She has often stated that she believes those who are seeking to change the law are creating confusion, resulting in court cases which they hope will ultimately secure a change in law. This would happen without Parliament even considering the matter, exactly as has happened in the Netherlands. She believes that the recent Lindsell case was an attempt to discredit the principle of double effect, whereby doctors are able to relieve the suffering of a patient even if this may have the foreseen but unintended effect of shortening a patient's life.

Ms Phillips sees the use of advance directives as a further tool through which the pro-euthanasia lobby will seek to change the law. Again, it will be open to the courts to interpret the law and the use of advance directives, and this is likely to prove a more fertile territory to those campaigning for a change in law than Parliament.

Interview

You have written a considerable amount about the Bland judgment, which in your mind was legalised euthanasia. This puts you at odds with five Law Lords and the British legal establishment. Can you outline how you come to see it as euthanasia?

The judges didn't believe that Bland was about euthanasia and went to some lengths to say that they had not produced a ruling which legalised euthanasia. They said this because, in my view, they made the casuistical distinctions over letting someone die and withdrawing feeding tubes. The main point was that the withdrawal of feeding tubes was not euthanasia because the feeding tube constituted artificial treatment, and it has been already established that one can withdraw treatment from someone who is terminally ill.

I thought that their judgment confused a number of things.

As I recall, I think it was Lord Mustill who said very clearly in the course of his speech in that judgment that, in his view, the judges had to realise that they were in fact being asked to cross a very significant legal line. I think that the distinction they were making about the use of the feeding tubes and letting someone die and all that, those distinctions were indeed casuistry.

The fact was that Tony Bland, like other PVS patients, was not dying. If he had been dying there would have been no problem, because it has always been established and accepted that if someone is dying then doctors are not only under no obligation to artificially prolong the process but, in the interests of the patient, should not prolong it artificially. The point was that Tony Bland wasn't dying: he was in a state of suspended animation, if you like, for the foreseeable future, and that situation was held to be intolerable to the people around him, to his parents in particular. While one absolutely sympathises with their predicament, it seemed to me that it was quite wrong to effectively say that someone's life should be ended in order to spare the suffering of someone else. That is not an acceptable principle for a society to base its activities on and that seemed to me to be what was going on there.

The fact was, he was not dying, and therefore what the doctors were asking permission to do was to take a course of action with the intention of bringing about his death, which otherwise was not going to happen. That to me is euthanasia. It is certainly an intention to end someone's life, which our law hitherto had been very clear should never be permitted. It was the great dividing line, and with that judgment they crossed over it, and so I think that judgment did actually legalise euthanasia.

Some have spoken of the Bland judgment as part of a conspiracy to legalise euthanasia. Isn't it more plausible that the case arose because medical treatment was not withdrawn at an earlier stage? Had antibiotics been withdrawn during an earlier infection, Tony Bland would have died from an infection or pneumonia and the case would never have arisen.

Yes, certainly, as I recall, it might have been the case that someone either panicked or was unsure about whether he should be treated with antibiotics. As I understand it that was a wrong panic because, if someone is dying, then a judgment can legitimately be made about whether it is in that person's interests to resuscitate them to stop them from dying. If they are actually dying it is a completely different matter from if they are not dying. If he had not been treated with antibiotics on that occasion when he was ill and when advice was sought, certainly what then happened would have been prevented. Clearly he wouldn't have been a PVS patient continuing to cause such distress to his family.

But the fact was, in ethical terms it was perfectly proper for the doctor not to have treated that infection. Indeed, if the Bland judgment had gone the other way and if the Law Lords had said that the feeding tubes could not be removed, almost certainly, as I understand it, in due course he would have succumbed to another infection. At that point his doctors would again have been perfectly within their legal and ethical rights not to have treated that infection and to have allowed the dying process, which would have commenced, to continue.

I think this is a distinction which, although fine, is very important, between allowing someone to die who is dying already and bringing about his death in circumstances where otherwise he would not have died. It is a line of huge importance because it all revolves around this business of intention, and you cannot intend to do something which is already happening. If someone is already dying you cannot intend to cause their death, because it is a process that has already started. If they are not dying, if you take an action which is going to cause their death then you are doing so because you intend to cause their death, which wouldn't otherwise happen.

There was a recent report under the chairmanship of a past President of the Royal College of Physicians which stated that it would be better to use the organs of people in PVS to assist others to have a higher quality of life rather than those in a condition where they will never feel, see, or think. Would it be much better to use their organs to enable those who need them to have a much better quality of life, possibly for thirty to forty years? What do you think of this approach?

You can only argue that it would be better for all concerned if the organs of a PVS patient were used to benefit someone else if you take the view that there is no intrinsic value to human life and that it is perfectly proper, and indeed desirable, to treat human beings as means rather than ends in themselves. I don't think either of those are sustainable in a civilised society.

I think that human beings must never be used as a means to an end, however noble the end may be. Once you go down that road then you can argue that all sorts of people's lives are of less consequence, of less importance, of less value to themselves, and that therefore they should also lose organs. You can literally start dismembering the human race on that basis, and, in a more general sense, if you regard human beings as meaningless to other people's happiness or good fortune then that opens up again a much bigger can of worms on the ethical front. You stop regarding each individual as equally precious, you start behaving in a completely unacceptable way.

Judges who refer to PVS patients as living corpses I think tell us more about their own state of ethical development than about the patient. You can't be a living corpse. It is a value judgment about the quality of that person's life. What judges are saying is that the quality of that person's life is so appalling they might as well be dead. Well, that's not an objective judgment. A corpse is dead; someone who is alive is not a corpse. If you treat someone who is alive as if they were a corpse then you have crossed not only a technical legal line, but you have crossed a moral and ethical line into a universe which I don't think any civilised society can properly inhabit. You are making judgments which it is not in your gift to make.

Sir Stephen Brown, the President of the Family Division of the High Court, said he was very happy to rule on these complex and sensitive cases. Under the current procedure, any of these cases would go before the High Court, which of course gave the ruling regarding Bland. Do you worry that the courts, and in particular the Family Division of the High Court, have such an important role in developing their ethical thinking on medical practice?

I worry about the way the courts are using this role. I don't worry that the courts have it, because I don't think there is a better way devised than having the courts ruling in these matters. Unless one were to legislate every five minutes as circumstances change and as science changes and technology changes, one has got to have a situation where the courts are interpreting law in the light of current developments.

What I think has gone wrong is that the judges, for a variety of reasons which I can touch on, have got the law wrong.

They have got it so wrong they have breached a fundamental principle which is the injunction in law against the deliberate and intentional taking of life. I think this is an absolute bulwark of law. They have made such a seismic mistake, the development that they are presiding over in case law is so potentially disastrous, that I think Parliament should legislate to restore the status quo. I think it should produce a short bill saying once again, emphatically and definitively, that intentional taking of life is wrong, in order to repair the breaches being made.

Why are the judges getting it so wrong? Partly it is because there is a generational thing that libertarian attitudes, value-free attitudes, value-neutral attitudes, which really got going about thirty years ago, have finally caught up with the higher reaches of the judiciary So, thirty years late, they finally got to where everybody else has been for the last thirty years and is now moving away from. Partly it is because they are, I suspect, themselves quite old and view with horror the prospect of losing their faculties in this way. I can't think of anything worse, as indeed many of us can't think of anything worse.

But I think the fundamental problem is that they are relying on the advice and information and observations of the people coming before them to argue the case. By definition, these cases are being brought by people who want to push the law towards giving permission to end life, and the judges are getting a very distorted view.

They are also getting a distorted view from the medical profession, which is being called as expert witnesses, because doctors themselves are confused and divided. Doctors themselves have a lamentable education in medical ethics and very often do not understand the distinctions which should revolve around intention. The judges are not being presented with information which I think bears both upon a proper ethical argument and upon what is actually going on. It seemed to me that, in the Bland case, the people involved in that case didn't accept that the majority of doctors operated by well-established legal and ethical guidelines. These permitted them to draw a distinction, or indeed encouraged them to draw a distinction, between deliberately taking a life and allowing it to end, and permitted them to operate where appropriate the doctrine of double effect. There were people involved in Bland who just didn't accept this was happening. It seemed to me they were just basically ignorant of the situation. So the judges are operating on prejudice and ignorance a great deal of the time and the result is that, as we saw in Bland, they have, I think, taken a huge leap in case law which has driven a coach and horses through the statute provision.

What about the recent Lindsell case? You will remember Annie Lindsell, who has since died from motor neurone disease, went to the High Court regarding the treatment that could be permitted when the disease advanced. The case caused considerable publicity. Do you think the Lindsell case was part of an orchestrated campaign by the euthanasia society to change the law using Annie Lindsell?

The case of Annie Lindsell was undoubtedly backed by the Voluntary Euthanasia Society. They put up a significant sum of money for her legal fees, they raised an additional amount of money through a campaign they organised. They had a kind of public information campaign, as it were, on the Internet and their spokesman popped up in all sorts of misleading ways as the case wore on.

It was never clear what was the intention of the case. Was it supposed to be fighting for her doctor to be able to give her an intentionally lethal dose of whatever drug it was when she wanted it, or was it, as she herself said, to allow the doctor to prescribe her enough of a pain-relieving or distress-relieving drug to relieve her pain and distress, even though that might have had the unintentional consequence of shortening her life? It was never clear which it was supposed to be, but if it was the latter, as she claimed, then it made very little sense. As the judge said, it was well accepted in law and in medical ethics that the doctrine of double effect could take place. There was no reason why she couldn't be prescribed the dose that she needed, even if it had the unintentional consequences of shortening her life. As I understand it, the amount of drugs that she needed to cope with any foreseeable pain and distress was actually not large enough to shorten her life. So the whole thing was a nonsense from start to finish in terms of the actual facts, and it did seem to me that, whether this was the intention or not, the consequence was to bamboozle the public. As a result a lot of people were left with the impression that, in the unfortunate event that they themselves might ever be in Annie Lindsell's position of suffering, the only way that they could guarantee that their doctor would prescribe them the drug they needed to stop their pain and distress was to be given a dose that would be fatal or potentially fatal.

This was a total confusion, because their doctors were always entitled and able to give them whatever drugs they would need to alleviate their pain and distress. This could happen even though the side-effect might be the unintentional shortening of their lives. There was still no need for this case and there was no need to have euthanasia to bring that situation about, but I think a lot of people were left after that case, or certainly while that case was going on, with the idea that in order to ensure that they would be looked after properly in their circumstances, society would need to legislate for euthanasia. Whether it was the intention of the Voluntary Euthanasia Society to bring about that state of confusion is a matter you should ask them, but it seems to me a very unfortunate muddle had been created in people's minds.

I should say that it was very odd that, at the time of the Annie Lindsell case, we suddenly found two or three or four doctors popping up who all said in the press that they had practised euthanasia and then said that actually what they were referring to was double effect.

Again, one had this complete confusion about euthanasia, that it was the same as double effect. It struck me as the most extraordinary coincidence of timing that this confusion was being perpetrated at the very same time that the Annie Lindsell case was perpetuating its own very similar confusion.

Experience from the Netherlands reveals clearly that changes in medical practice can happen quickly, even without statute law being changed. Do you think that in ten years' time we will have legalised euthanasia exactly as is happening in Holland? Do you believe that the courts will take further opportunities to push the boundaries of the current position to such an extent that the law as it stands is untenable?

As to whether we will have euthanasia in ten years' time, I think that we could well drift into it – indeed, we are drifting into it. It's a kind of creative flux situation in which the drip effect of these court cases means that the agenda will simply be pushed on through court cases. We've had Bland, we've had several similar cases since Bland, despite the fact that some people who have been diagnosed as PVS have actually exhibited some signs of consciousness subsequently. I am sure very soon there will be a growing clamour which says, 'Well, actually starving a patient to death (which is precisely what happens now in these PVS cases) is inhumane, and wouldn't it be much more civilised to actually administer euthanasia by lethal injection?' If one is on this slippery slope and has made this logical and ethical leap then, of course, that does follow, and so bit by bit we are going to see this agenda being pushed forward.

At the same time I think the public is deeply confused. I see at the moment on the horizon no institutional counter to that confusion, and I see no Parliamentarians who are making a cognant and intellectually coherent case. Certainly people associated with the hospice movement are making it, but their voices are not that loud. They don't have the muscle of Britain's institutions behind them. I see the Law Commission proceeding in a value-neutral, moral relativist path which seeks to legalise euthanasia by the back door, without actually legislating, through living wills and through giving the Bland judgment statutory effect. I don't see Parliamentarians trying to counter this. I don't see lawyers trying to counter this. I don't see (apart from some slightly ambiguous references by the BMA) doctors, by and large, trying to counter it. I don't see a great campaign trying to educate the public in ethics and medical law to counter this trend at all. If it's left as it is, then yes, in ten years' time we will undoubtedly have got to where Holland is. I only hope that sufficient people of sound ethical mind and a bit of common sense will be able to get together to educate the public as to what's happening and what the consequences are going to be.

Can we touch on the issue of advance directives – whether or not you are in favour of writing down personally in advance what treatment you would or would not like in fifteen or twenty years' time. There have been a variety of bills drafted both by backbenchers and by the Law

Commission with a view to enhancing the status of such directives. Have you written an advance directive? Do you think it's a good idea?

Personally I have not written an advance directive and wouldn't do so. I think there is a profound logical flaw in advance directives. I don't think there is anything wrong in letting doctors know what one's wishes are; the more information, the better, so they can be equipped. But the idea that one can ever seek to bind a doctor, the idea that I can know now what the state of medical science might be in fifteen or twenty years' time, what my domestic circumstances might be in fifteen to twenty years' time . . . The idea that I may be incapacitated within my useless body with my mind still functioning is a horrific prospect, there's no doubt about that. I'm as prone to being horrified about that as anyone else, but I could not presume to know what I would feel like if I were in that situation. I am told that people believe when they're healthy that life in that situation would be insupportable, but when it actually comes to it, the desire to hang on to life is so strong they actually don't wish to relinquish it. I don't know whether I would be in that category or not. I couldn't possibly predict and I wouldn't seek to predict it, I simply don't know. So I would never be so foolish as to lay down in advance binding directions to doctors as to how I should be treated based on circumstances which I can't possible predict.

Worries have been expressed that the worldwide pro-euthanasia groups are the most ardent proponents of advance directives. Do you think they promote them because they will be used as a tool to bring forward euthanasia?

I think they are undoubtedly being used to bring euthanasia in by the back door. The Voluntary Euthanasia Chairman was quoted some years ago as saying that the British Parliament would never legislate for euthanasia because it will never have the bottle to do that, and I think he was entirely correct. It would be astonishing to me if a Parliament with any government in power would legislate for euthanasia. However, I think the forces pushing for euthanasia are extremely strong, and they are very strong in Britain's institutions at the moment. I think that they will go to great lengths to bring it about by covert means. They have learned the lessons from the Netherlands, and I think that's precisely the way they're going.

I think we're going to see more and more cases brought to court in order to push case law on. Unless the Law Commission suddenly reforms itself, I think we can rely on the Law Commission to push this whole agenda along and I think that the euthanasia lobby is very formidably organised and very entrenched in the Civil Service and in the higher echelons of the judiciary. Like all good lobbying groups it knows what it is dealing with, knows how to influence public opinion and is going to use its best wiles to do precisely that. So I think advance directives are a shrewd move as far as it's concerned, because they don't sound like euthanasia, they sound eminently reasonable. After all, we all want to have control over our own lives and over our own deaths. It's only if you start thinking about it in some depth that you begin to see any of these drawbacks. In such an emotive area, I would think that not many people will think about these things in that depth unless there is a concerted counter-attack which draws to public attention the likely consequences and the broader agenda which is at work here.

Lord Walton of Detchant

Biographical details

Lord Walton has enjoyed a successful career as one of the world's leading neurologists. A former Professor of Neurology at Newcastle University Hospitals, former President of the BMA, the Royal Society of Medicine and the World Federation of Neurologists, his expertise is renowned through the world. He is the author of numerous papers and publications regarding neurology. Lord Walton was created a Life Peer in 1989 for his services to medicine and sits as a cross-bencher in the House of Lords.

In 1993 Lord Walton was approached to chair a House of Lords Select Committee inquiry into the issue of euthanasia. The Committee of fourteen met for over a year calling evidence, interviewing leading groups and individuals and drawing up a unanimous report which was against any change of law legalising euthanasia. The report of the Walton Committee has been a primary source of reference to many studying the issues and has had considerable influence on the long-term development of government policy.

Introductory comments

It was an obvious choice to appoint Lord Walton of Detchant to chair the House of Lords Select Committee on Medical

Ethics for its investigation into euthanasia. As a neurologist he had both the knowledge and the expertise to find a way through the dilemmas raised by the Bland case. However, at the start, the establishment of the Committee was not without some controversy, with a number of Lords expressing disquiet over both the membership of the Committee and the terms of reference. Despite some criticism in the press, Lord Walton managed the task of securing a unanimous report, something which is by no means guaranteed of Parliamentary Select Committees.

Being a neurologist, Lord Walton was only too aware that as medical science becomes increasingly complex so do ethical decisions regarding questions of treatment, and none more so than in the area of patients suffering from brain damage following a traumatic accident. For some, the withdrawal of a life-support machine reveals that the brain stem, that part of the brain responsible for driving the heart, lungs, etc., is no longer viable, and the patient dies. Brain stem death is currently effectively equated with the definition of death, as the patient's life is not viable without artificial support for ventilation.

For others, the withdrawal of life support reveals that the brain stem is functioning normally, and so the patient survives. This leaves the healthcare team with the highly specialist task of ascertaining the degree of activity in the cerebral cortex, that part of the brain responsible for consciousness. The medical profession has developed tests to diagnose the different conditions of the cerebral cortex, and a vocabulary of terms has been established: 'coma', 'locked-in syndrome' and 'persistent vegetative state'. Lord Walton helpfully defines these terms at the start of the interview.

It is patients in a persistent vegetative state who provide the dilemmas so relevant to the euthanasia debate, which are discussed in depth with Lord Walton during the interview.

The main ethical dilemma concerns diagnosis. How can one be sure that the patient is in a permanent or persistent vegetative state? Is recovery from such a condition possible, or could the patient be merely in a temporary coma? Could the patient be conscious of all that is going on around but not able to communicate effectively? How do you account for the noises that patients make, the eye movement and other reactions? These are some of the dilemmas of diagnosis for patients in a persistent vegetative state.

Diagnosis is vital, for it has a bearing on the type of treatment and care which should be offered to such patients. While most people agree that it is appropriate to withdraw medical treatment from patients in a persistent vegetative state, such as the provision of antibiotics and initiating new medical procedures, it is the question of feeding which causes the problems.

Lord Walton is in favour of withdrawing food and fluid from patients in a persistent vegetative state, but is against euthanasia. He explains his thinking in the interview, accounting for the position he has taken. His Committee would not unanimously accept his opinion and instead it ruled that a growing acceptance of the practice of withdrawing medical treatment from patients in a persistent vegetative state should make questions over the withdrawal of food and fluid unnecessary. The Committee agreed that if antibiotic regimes and other treatment were stopped at an earlier stage, then patients in a persistent vegetative state would be likely to die sooner, rather than later from the withdrawal of food and fluid.

Other matters are raised during the interview but the issue of the provision of food and water, the matter which came close to dividing his Committee, is the central focus of the discussion.

Interview

One of the issues which will be discussed in the euthanasia debate is the central concern of the Bland judgment. Is it appropriate to withdraw nutrition from a patient which will result in their life being ended? Could such a course of action be in their best interest? As a neurologist you must have seen some quite distressing cases of people who seem to have no quality of life. From your experience of these cases, I wondered if perhaps you could give me an indication as to whether or not you totally supported the Bland judgment.

I begin by saying that it is very important to be precise in your neurological definitions. The age-old belief that death is synonymous with the heart stopping has been refined with advances in medical technology. It's now generally accepted, in the UK and many other countries, that brain stem death as defined in the criteria laid down by the Medical Royal Colleges can effectively be equated with death.

An individual who is brain stem dead cannot live without mechanically assisted artificial support and ventilation and demonstrates absence of many forms of reflex activity. Once the respirator stops, the heart soon stops beating, and if those diagnostic criteria are confirmed by two experienced physicians then it is acceptable to stop the respirator and arrange where appropriate to remove organs for transplantation.

Now let us be clear about other distinctions. Coma is loss of consciousness from which the patient cannot be aroused. The locked-in syndrome is a curious condition in which the patient is conscious and alert but paralysed in all four limbs and unable to speak or swallow. Communication is possible only through blinking or voluntary eye movements. This is a very rare condition, but the patient is totally sentient and of course in those patients there is no question in my view of withdrawal of life support. Complete or partial recovery from coma is common; there may be no permanent disability or the effects may be mild or severe depending on the duration of the coma and its cause. Recovery from the locked-in syndrome is virtually unknown.

The vegetative state has been well defined, I think, by the American Medical Association. It is a condition in which the body cyclically awakens and sleeps but expresses no behavioural or cerebral metabolic evidence of possessing cognitive functions or of being able to respond in a learned manner to external events and stimuli.

So far as the vegetative state is concerned, it is a medical diagnosis based upon clinical observation. It implies death or disjunction of the cerebral cortex with the preservation of brain stem function. A vegetative state can be diagnosed at an instant in time but the persistent or permanent vegetative state is one which has continued for at least one month. I prefer myself not to diagnose PVS unless it has lasted for twelve months. Now contrary to what Keith Andrews from Putney will say, I am unaware of any instances of recovery from fully developed PVS. I think that some patients who have been so diagnosed did not fulfil all the diagnostic criteria which have now been reaffirmed by the Conference of Colleges. So I think that definitions are absolutely crucial and I have seen many such cases over the years; there is no doubt that some severely brain-injured individuals who subsequently show partial recovery, even a very few complete recovery, from a state of prolonged coma were not in a fully vegetative state. And there, I think, is where I disagree with Keith Andrews.

I agree with you that definition and diagnosis are very important. I was reading in the supplementary written evidence to your Report of a sixty-one-year-old lady who was in PVS for three years. Yet contrary to expectations, according to the respected physician Dr Keith Andrews, she made a recovery which enabled her to read, to write, to feed, to walk and to speak.

I don't accept that she was in PVS. Of course, I didn't see the patient. All I can say is that those who I believe fulfil the full criteria have not, in my experience, shown any significant degree of recovery. I did go to the National Centre for Neuro-disability in Putney and saw some of Dr Andrews' patients; while I accepted that many of them had been severely brain injured and had been comatose for a long period, I did not believe personally that they were cases of true PVS. I know he will disagree, but that is my personal view.

So would you share the view of one eminent lawyer who stated that Mr Bland's 'spirit had left him'?

Yes, yes.

Would you agree in essence that therefore Mr Bland was dead?

No, not dead, because his brain stem was still functioning. There was no doubt of that at all. He still had a functioning cardiovascular system. But of course, his cerebral cortex was dead and there is no doubt, therefore, in my view, that he did not have any knowledge or awareness whatever of his surroundings. Also, we should look at what certain other people said in commenting on the case. The Patients'

Association said that effectively a person in a persistent vegetative state, or what the Colleges prefer to call a permanent vegetative state, has finished their life as a human being. Some of our witnesses before the Select Committee suggested that in such cases the quality of life is not just poor but non-existent; I think I would accept that.

He was alive, but that part of the brain, namely the cerebral cortex, through which all of the functions which distinguish human beings from lower animals are controlled, was dead, and therefore he was really little more than a functioning cardiovascular system. After all, he could not swallow, he had to be tube-fed; he could breathe and his cardiovascular system was working, but that was effectively all. There was nothing else in his behaviour or in his responses or lack of responses which demonstrated any kind of awareness of his surroundings.

And in those circumstances you think it was justifiable to withdraw food and water, even though surely the intention was to end his life, or whatever phrase one would use to describe his state?

Now this is the question which exercised my Committee greatly. After all, the High Court and the Court of Appeal and the Law Lords, each looking at the case of Tony Bland, all came to the conclusion that food and water, nutrition and hydration, if given by an invasive method – i.e. by a feeding tube – was medical treatment. They concluded, as many others have done, that there was no obligation to continue with medical treatment which could have no long-term beneficial effect upon the individual in relation to restoration of awareness or other brain functions. So they came to the conclusion that it was proper for the feeding tube to be withdrawn. But, of course, they added the caveat that they were not expecting this case necessarily to create a precedent, in that all similar cases would have to be referred in the future to the High Court for individual consideration, which is actually what has happened. In my Committee there was a dispute on this issue because there were certain organisations and some individuals, particularly in the nursing profession and in the organisation Life, for example, who took the view that food and fluid are a basic human right, however administered, and should not be withdrawn under any circumstances.

Indeed, nurses and some others on our Committee viewed this as a basic human right. I would have thought that the majority shared my own personal opinion, not the eventual agreed opinion of the Committee, that it is medical treatment if in order to give food and fluid you have to invade the body by putting a tube down into the stomach. I regard that as medical treatment, as the Law Lords concluded. Therefore they decided that, like other forms of medical treatment, it could be withdrawn. If we as a Committee had disagreed and continued to disagree on that point, in order finally to come to a resolution we would have had to hold a division, because there are no minority reports on Select Committees. But in the end we got around the problem by saying that if the consultant in question had been able to get permission to withdraw antibiotics at an earlier stage then the effect would have been ultimately the same. Dr Jim Howe asked for permission from the court to withdraw both the feeding tube and the antibiotics. If he had just sought permission to withdraw antibiotics nobody could have had any objections, and I think the outcome would have been identical. So in the end our conclusion in our report was that there was no obligation to continue with medical treatment if it added nothing to the well-being of the person as an individual.

Surely describing nutrition and hydration as 'artificial' if fed through a tube and calling it medical treatment was merely a convenient way of justifying its withdrawal? Current law states clearly that medical treatment can be withdrawn where it will be of no benefit. But is feeding really medical treatment? Placing a naso-gastric tube into a patient is undertaken by nurses who very often train the relatives of long-term patients to undertake the procedure.

I regard it as an invasion of the body. The fact that many people are being taught to take their own blood pressure and that many nurses do procedures which they were never allowed to do in my student days is now accepted. However, I do not regard invasive medical procedures as part of nursing care.

Articles were written in the press at the time of the case suggesting that the Bland judgment was the first legalised case of voluntary euthanasia. Would you agree with this?

No, I would not. There is, in my opinion, contrary to what the philosophers have to say, a very striking distinction between killing and letting die. Killing is a deliberate act where the intention is to kill; there are many circumstances where there is no clear distinction between killing and letting die. In every situation which we discussed with many different organisations, there was a clear recognition that there are circumstances when there is no obligation to continue with medical treatment which is fruitless and can do nothing in the longer term for the individual. So I believe that that is letting die, that is a decision to withdraw or withhold treatment, and I do not regard that as euthanasia, just as I do not regard double effect as euthanasia. Voluntary euthanasia is an act of deliberate termination of the patient's life at the request of the individual, with the intention to do nothing other than terminate that patient's life. Non-voluntary euthanasia is carrying out a similar act in an incompetent individual. Involuntary euthanasia is taking a decision to end the life of an individual who is physically competent to give permission or to withhold permission; and that, of course, is abhorrent in all civilised societies. My belief is that withholding treatment or withdrawing treatment when it is shown to be futile is quite different from a deliberate act of intentional killing. In the same way, double effect means that if it is necessary for a doctor, in order to relieve pain, distress and suffering, to give such doses of medication that this has the secondary consequence of shortening life, that is acceptable in medical practice and the law, but the intention must not be to kill.

Do you consider that the current practice in the Netherlands provides an adequate reason for not legalising euthanasia in this country?

My understanding is that in Holland more than one doctor has now been prosecuted for practising euthanasia without the appropriate criteria and safeguards having being fulfilled; I think there has been a certain pulling-back from the brink, particularly in relation to non-voluntary cases. I have been concerned because it seemed to me that it had become a policy, widely practised and condoned, that not all cases were being reported to the coroner according to the legal requirements.

Another issue which exercised your Committee was that of advance directives or, as they are sometimes known, living wills. Both the last government and the present administration have considered the possibility of legislation on the matter.

In common law there is no doubt that the advance directive or living will is being recognised increasingly, and you will have seen the BMA's report, which I commend. I think it is a very sensible and well-written report and it is one which I would accept wholly. My only concern about the living will is that if it were to be made totally legally binding, without any exceptions, someone signing a living will might reach the situation of becoming incompetent in 2010, at which time the situation would have changed totally and certain treatment which would be thought inappropriate in 1999 might, because of advances in medicine, have become very appropriate. Now this could be readily overcome if the people who sign living wills, as I have done, were to update them every four or five years, but human beings being what they are, I suspect that most people having signed a living will hand it to their general practitioner and forget all about it. Updating them is not going to be something which is very easy; thus I think it is very important that there should be room for certain exceptions which would mostly relate to major developments in medical knowledge and medical science. Having said that, I accept the principle.

The other thing which I would say is that if the Lord Chancellor has been properly quoted in the press, we were disappointed, frankly, that our recommendations in the report on the permanent vegetative state or, as we called it then, the persistent vegetative state, were not accepted, or at least have not been implemented. We recommended first that if a course of action was totally acceptable to the relatives of the individual, to the carers, medical and nursing staff and others, and there was absolutely no dispute about the validity of withdrawing feeding by a tube, as in the Tony Bland case, that should be allowed legally without reference to the High Court. But if there were any disagreement whatever between the nurses, the doctors or the family, we recommended the establishment of locally based tribunals which would be able to make a rapid decision, based upon the principles of the Court of Protection. Indeed, that was something that the English and Scottish Law Commissions both recommended, but no movement has yet taken place towards the establishment of such tribunals, which would avoid the necessity, expense and delay involved in going to the High Court in every case. So I am hoping that the Lord Chancellor will bring forward a bill which will establish such tribunals to handle these cases at a local level.

Returning to the issue of living wills, you don't feel that there is a potential clash between personal autonomy and what the law deems is permissible and not permissible? For example, what would happen if somebody, on the issue of food and water, wrote a living will asking for something which technically wasn't legal or might be a grey area? In the increasingly litigious society in which we live, doctors could find themselves accused of battery on the one hand or negligence on the other.

I think that is an extremely difficult problem and it is something which the legislation, if it is to be brought in, must address. At the moment such directives are not legally binding by statute, though any doctor failing to comply with the terms of a living will at present would have to justify his or her actions. I would have thought that if the individual had said that they did not want to be artificially fed but that proved to be contrary to the existing law, then the doctor would have every justification in ignoring what was said and laid down.

The same as if they asked for a lethal injection?

Absolutely – they could not do that either. So I think this is something that will have to be very carefully examined when the legislation is drafted.

Do you think people could be forced into signing living wills? An elderly relative, becoming frail and infirm, burdened with the worry and anxiety of becoming a nuisance, might feel pressured into signing a directive.

That is an anxiety, of course, that some people have, but of course such documents have to be witnessed by someone who is independent before they actually have any legal force. The other issue about which I have just given evidence is the question as to whether an individual would have the right under a living will to recommend that their sperm or ova might be used for the benefit of their partner. I am thinking of the Diane Blood case, where she sought the court's permission to use her husband's sperm after his death in order to conceive. That is another issue which is going to be a matter of concern over the next few years and about which the Human Fertilisation and Embryology Authority and the Department of Health have been deliberating.

Do you think that the living will debate has been cornered by the pro-euthanasia lobby, who obviously advertise and aggressively market the directives? Perhaps a more effective approach to deciding on appropriate treatment, discussed a lot during your Committee, involves multi-disciplinary healthcare, with all members of the healthcare team in consultation with the patient where possible and the relatives. Won't advance directives lead to less communication between the patient and doctor, as they will abide by the directive rather than discussing and coming to a mutually agreeable position?

The Committee recommended, irrespective of living wills, that if the whole healthcare team were of one mind re a PVS patient they shouldn't have to go to the High Court, but that still hasn't been enshrined in legislation. We recommended that if there was any difference of opinion the case would have to go to a tribunal. But, of course, if there had been a living will the healthcare team would have great difficulty, as I have said, in failing to comply with the living will provided its provisions were legally acceptable, and if they did fail to comply they would have to justify their actions.

How are these living wills going to work in practice? Only 20 per cent get round to signing a proper will, and here we are advocating another will which could have a far more dramatic impact. How would you define what is a living will? What if a physician was faced with the back of an envelope with a few scribbled notes – would they be obliged to abide by it?

I think they have to be very properly prepared and drawn up; there are forms which are available, not least from the Voluntary Euthanasia Society and from other organisations, which are very careful to specify the circumstances in which an individual would not wish to be kept alive. So I am not unhappy about their contents. I certainly would not be happy about someone scribbling notes on the back of an envelope even if this were witnessed; that is another issue where the legal definition, structure and content of these living wills is going to have to be very carefully addressed.

Looking to the wider issue of euthanasia and the way the debate is likely to progress in the next five or ten years, do you think that euthanasia has had its day and there is now general worldwide opinion against it, or do you think that it will be legalised further in the next five or ten years?

I have no doubt whatever that the highly articulate and able and, I think, sincere proponents of voluntary euthanasia will continue their campaign. When I think of people like the Ludovic Kennedys of this world and many of the other people who support the Voluntary Euthanasia Society, I think they will continue their efforts in the hope of slowly wearing down the opposition. My own belief is that, within this country in the foreseeable future, opposition will continue to be effective. I would only add, relating to many of the cases that are referred to in the press (there was a notable case recently in my native city of Newcastle upon Tyne), that a number of doctors have come forward saying that they practise euthanasia. I don't believe they do; I believe they have been practising double effect and been doing so for many years, and I don't see any problem over that, as I said at the outset, provided the intention is not to kill.

Take, for example, the Lindsell case. I understand that she was not asking for euthanasia; she made that quite clear. What she was asking for was double effect; she was quoted as having said that her doctors accepted that they could give drugs to relieve pain even if they had a secondary consequence of shortening life. However, they had not said that they would give drugs which would relieve distress and suffering, which is what she was seeking. In our report it was very clear that we talked about double effect for the relief of pain, and also to relieve distress and suffering. To take another example, if Dr Cox, the rheumatologist, had given his patient massive doses of a sedative such as diazepam or one of its derivatives, so that the patient had gone quietly to sleep despite having intolerable pain, I do not think any problem would have arisen. It is because he gave her a particular substance intravenously which could have no other consequence than to stop her heart that he was charged and convicted.

The Liberal Democrats have called for a Royal Commission as a result of a recent party conference motion. Do you think such an approach is appropriate and necessary?

No, I don't, personally, because I thought that we had gone into this whole issue in sufficient depth in the House of Lords Select Committee; of course, others may well disagree. After all, it is more than four years since our report was debated in May 1994 in the House and it may be that there are those who feel that the situation should be reviewed. I myself think it would be premature to do so.

Dr Peter Admiraal

Biographical details

Dr Peter Admiraal is a retired anaesthetist who for many years worked in a hospital in Delft, during which time he practised euthanasia. He was tried in 1985 for assisting in the death of a patient who was suffering from multiple sclerosis. The case collapsed as the patient was deemed to be suffering unbearably.

Since then Dr Admiraal has become one of the strongest supporters of the practice of euthanasia in the Netherlands and spends considerable time touring Europe lecturing and debating the current practice.

Dr Admiraal is interested in medical ethics and is a member of the International Academy of Humanists. Since retiring he spends his time lecturing, and relaxing at his home in Switzerland.

Introductory comments

The present situation in the Netherlands warrants a detailed interview on the thinking and practice behind the current law. Discussions were undertaken with a number of medical practitioners in the Netherlands, including Dr Admiraal, who is recognised throughout Europe as one of the most outspoken proponents of euthanasia. He himself was the subject of a

118

court case in 1985 concerning a woman suffering from multiple sclerosis who was referred to him at his hospital in Rotterdam after her own hospital refused to comply with her wish for euthanasia. Dr Admiraal agreed to her wish and assisted her to die. In the ensuing court case, Dr Admiraal was not convicted, on the grounds that he undertook an emergency act.

The interview follows some of the historical background to the current position in the Netherlands, where euthanasia remains a criminal act under the penal code but is legally permitted under certain circumstances.

This situation arose following a number of court cases in the 1970s and 1980s which reflected judicial lenience towards doctors practising euthanasia. Following the courts' endorsement of euthanasia and the support of the Royal Dutch Medical Association, in 1993 the Dutch Parliament voted to allow voluntary euthanasia for the incurably ill who were suffering a perpetual, unbearable and hopeless situation. The Parliament endorsed guidelines stipulating that the patient must be in a clear state of mind, repeating a request for euthanasia, and in an intolerable situation. Guidelines also stress that a second medical opinion ought to be sought and detailed accounts kept at every stage.

In the interview Dr Admiraal is critical of the current legal position in the Netherlands, which forces a doctor to criminalise himself. When a practitioner commits euthanasia, he informs a local coroner of an unnatural death. The coroner in turn informs a prosecutor. The prosecutor will then investigate the case, and normally the doctor is given permission to send the body for burial. Dr Admiraal accuses this legal position of being 'very silly', where a doctor is being asked to confess to a crime for which he is then pardoned.

During the interview the issue of the Remmelink Report

is raised. The Remmelink Committee was established in 1990 by the Dutch government. Headed by the Attorney General of the Supreme Court, J. Remmelink, it was to research into the practice of euthanasia in the Netherlands. It reported in 1991, revealing that of 128,786 deaths in the Netherlands in 1990, 1.8 per cent were due to voluntary euthanasia, 0.3 per cent to assisted suicide and 0.8 per cent to life-terminating acts without explicit and persistent request. It revealed that euthanasia was practised on more than three thousand people in the Netherlands in 1990, and in 1,030 of those cases it was not voluntary. A later review was undertaken for the Dutch government in 1995, which revealed that there were 900 deaths from euthanasia in that year which were not voluntary.

In the interview Dr Admiraal admits that he himself failed to inform the prosecutor of a case he undertook and that 60 per cent of cases of euthanasia in the Netherlands are not reported. He blames the current law for doctors failing to criminalise themselves, and states that often medical practitioners are too upset to report the case. In addition, he believes that many doctors see it as good medical practice which should not involve a criminal procedure.

On the question of palliative care Dr Admiraal refutes those who believe that there is little palliative care in the Netherlands. He states that he himself has been involved in palliative care for many years, establishing it in the Netherlands in 1973. He outlines the interaction between his own department and the work of St Christopher's Hospice in Sydenham.

However, Dr Admiraal believes that euthanasia should be an option for patients as palliative care is of limited significance in a small number of cases. He is highly critical of hospice doctors in the United Kingdom who increase the dosage of drugs to avoid patients suffocating or being in pain at the end of life. Whereas he would advocate euthanasia, hospice doctors in Britain believe that the dosage of palliatives should be increased with the foreseen but unintended effect of shortening a patient's life. While Dr Admiraal describes such doctors in positive terms, he suggests that such actions are hypocritical.

The interview touches on the Chabot case of 1994 where the Dutch Supreme Court convicted but declined to punish a psychiatrist for assisting the death of a patient who was physically healthy. The Dutch Supreme Court upheld the decision by Dr Chabot to administer a fatal injection to a woman suffering from depression. Dr Admiraal believes that doctors should have the right to assist patients to die even if they are not in a terminal condition but are suffering, for instance from depression. The position of the patient needs to be checked and other colleagues drawn into an assessment. Dr Admiraal feels that where a patient's unbearable suffering cannot be made bearable it is 'ridiculous' for a doctor to state that the suffering is bearable. While Dr Admiraal will not accept involuntary euthanasia, stating that it is clearly murder, he will accept non-voluntary euthanasia, where a patient is unable to request euthanasia as a result of being in a coma. Dr Admiraal believes there is a place for it and admits to having undertaken such practice.

Throughout the interview Dr Admiraal gives an indication of the ethical basis for his position on euthanasia. He believes strongly in the principle of self-determination arising out of his adherence to humanistic principles. Tracing the development of ethical thinking over the centuries, he believes that euthanasia will become acceptable and that future generations will be surprised at our reticence to practise euthanasia. He admires the Dutch practitioners who made such a stance against the Nazis' attempt to force Dutch doctors into practising euthanasia. However, he believes that, in today's world, euthanasia is the last dignified act of palliative care.

Interview

Euthanasia continues to be at the forefront of public debate in England. In the light of your own court case in the 1980s, perhaps you might like to comment on the development of the issue in the UK.

Dutch law is very different from the English system. In the Netherlands, practising euthanasia and assisted suicide is forbidden. For euthanasia you can face a maximum of twelve years in prison, and with assisted suicide a maximum of four.

Under the current legal framework the doctor is always guilty, and it is still illegal. It is still the same law, which may be changed next year. It is very different from Germany, Switzerland, Austria and countries where assisted suicide is not illegal. There you can do that without problems, but here it is all illegal.

I told the prosecutor I did euthanasia in 1982. Prior to that we had had a few court cases of euthanasia. By that time the Royal Dutch Medical Association had accepted euthanasia as a possibility. During those years efforts were made to find a legal framework and a jurisdiction was established by a number of pro-euthanasia cases.

The first case was in 1972; it was a doctor killing her mother. She got a one-week suspended sentence, and that was all. The next case was one or two years later. It was a layman and he was also found guilty, but again the court accepted it. After a brief pause three cases followed rapidly. The first case was a young doctor. He had allegedly killed fifteen elderly cancer patients in their old people's home.

He could not prove that the patients had ever asked for euthanasia. He did not discuss it with the nurses or sister or other colleagues, so he was quite alone. He was taken into prison and accused of murder because he could not prove it was euthanasia. Everybody believed it was euthanasia, but because he did not speak to anybody they could not prove it so he was accused of murder. That was a famous case because he was nine months in prison.

There was another case of a doctor who did kill a lady in her nineties, simply because she didn't want to live any longer. She had a lot of complaints but had no terminal disease, so she was not in her dying phase. Until now all the other cases were terminal cancer patients, so this was the first with a non-terminal non-cancer patient.

Then came my case, a lady suffering from multiple sclerosis, which was also not terminal. She could have lived for months; we did not know. I did euthanasia because she could not swallow, and one of her problems was that if she should aspirate food she would suffocate. She refused to have a stomach tube so we accepted that as a group in our hospital.

The Minister of Justice decided to make a court case of my patient to see what should be the outcome of the three cases. The verdict came in 1985, within a few weeks for all three cases. The young doctor, as I said, was accused of murder and they wanted to sentence him to eight years in prison, but then his lawyer proved there was a fault in the whole process. He did not prove he didn't do it, but they had to stop the prosecution and actually he got a lot of money later on because he was nine months in prison. The second was the old doctor, who had already gone to the appeal court, and now he was sent back to a normal court for a second appeal. The outcome of his case was that they accepted he did euthanasia on the old lady and they accepted there was unbearable suffering, so they stopped prosecuting.

The same happened in my case: they concluded she was in unbearable suffering and there was no way out, so they stopped prosecuting. I was not set free; they simply stopped prosecuting.

Euthanasia is illegal, so they can never say it's OK, but they can stop prosecuting. Officially the outcome was that the prosecutor said that I should have asked a neurologist and a psychiatrist for a decision, but they found that I was responsible enough to do it on my own as a doctor under these circumstances. Today you have to ask another doctor, always, in all cases.

What is important about these cases is that it was accepted in both the terminal phase and in the non-terminal phase, and more and more it became clear that if you prove, as a doctor or with two doctors, that there is unbearable suffering, euthanasia is acceptable.

It's complicated, but in our law, while it is illegal, if you can prove that you were in a situation where you had to make a choice between two ways out, then sometimes you can do the illegal in an emergency situation. They simply say, 'It's illegal, but for you there was no other possibility.' Compare it with a person driving along a canal who cannot park their car. They see someone drowning and save him, having parked their car illegally. The authorities are never going to prosecute a person for parking there. As a doctor I am in a very difficult position, to obey the law or to do what the patients ask. In the Netherlands they say you can do what the patient wants. That's still so.

So what do you put on the death certificate?

I tell the coroner that there was unnatural death, a case of euthanasia. So he comes and checks the body and tells the prosecutor he has a case of euthanasia. The prosecutor will then write to me as the doctor and usually says I can bury the body.

Under the current rules he will send his advice to the Attorney General and they will decide. Sometimes it takes over a year to hear that the Assembly of the Attorney General accepted it. That can be sometimes very disappointing and upsetting because you don't hear the outcome for a few months.

The failing of the current system is that doctors have to confess to doing a criminal thing. I think the European Court should say we don't accept that. It cannot force somebody to criminalise himself. The law is being changed, and after that the coroner will have to call the prosecutor. He has to give permission to bury the body, and then you will be visited as a doctor by a committee of a doctor, a jurist and a psychologist. They will go through the case and in the end they will accept it and tell the prosecutor that they accept it.

So it is a kind of law which tells you how to do a crime. It's very silly, but that's where we are at. The law will say how you can commit a crime.

One of the points made in a recent book about euthanasia in the Netherlands is that euthanasia needs to be legalised because it is impossible to know, under the current procedures, what exactly is going on in terms of the number of cases there are.

If we want to admit we have done euthanasia officially we are obliged to do that. In the MS case I went to the coroner and told him I had done a case of euthanasia, so he reported it to the prosecutor.

Your case has been cited as an example that euthanasia was being practised but not initially reported. Had you been practising euthanasia prior to this MS case and what had you been putting on the death certificate?

I did report another case before and I didn't hear anything, so I thought that they accepted it. Later on, with the second case, it transpired that a coroner did not report to the prosecutor, giving me the false impression that everything was accepted. So I was upset that suddenly the police were there.

You qualified as an anaesthetist in 1961. Between then and 1985, did you undertake other cases?

The first case was in 1969, but I didn't tell the prosecutor, and why should I? Today 60 per cent don't tell the prosecutor that they do euthanasia, they simply fill in 'natural death'. The majority of the doctors in the Netherlands don't tell the prosecutor they are doing it.

Why is that?

There are many reasons. First, a doctor does not want to criminalise himself. He doesn't accept the fact that it is against the constitution to do so. Another reason can be that he is upset about another colleague's case lasting for over a year and he is still doubting what they will do. It can be a medical secret between the patient and the doctor. Mostly they say, 'I am not a criminal and it's good medical care and I will never report it to the prosecutor.'

What the government is doing is to try and find a way where more and more doctors will report it, because they want to know how many cases there are. In the famous

Remmelink Report we actually know we have about 4,500 cases a year, and we know exactly what they have reported and that's about 40 per cent. I have always said it is ridiculous to control a doctor after euthanasia, because the patient is buried. You have to control it before.

They are likely to appoint doctors who you can ask before doing euthanasia, so you can be within the law asking an independent colleague for advice. Such a doctor may be an expert in palliative care, for instance, so he can go through the whole process and check that you have proposed the best treatment. If he concludes that it is acceptable before the patient has died, this makes the Committee's role afterwards rather obsolete.

From 1969 to 1985, sixteen years, you said you had practised euthanasia prior to your case. Was it a regular occurrence in your medical practice, and what criteria did you use to decide that it was appropriate in those cases where you practised it? Was it voluntary or non-voluntary? Was it terminal illness or non-terminal illness?

I was working in a hospital and I was practically only dealing with cancer patients. We had an average of one hundred patients with cancer in our hospital per year and from the beginning we did around 8 per cent euthanasia. Now in 1990 and 1995 the Remmelink Report has proved that it is still around 8–10 per cent of all cancer patients asking for euthanasia. Of all our euthanasia cases in the Netherlands, more than 80 per cent have cancer. The remaining group of about 20 per cent are equally divided between Aids, neurological diseases and elderly patients.

I didn't look after Aids patients, but we did care for neurological patients, the MS patient being an example. Mostly the whole group were cancer patients and were in a terminal phase. We had very good terminal care in the hospital. I visited Cecily Saunders in 1968 in St Christopher's Hospice to see what she was doing and to tell her our experience with a brand new morphine-like drug for painkilling. I came back to my hospital and reported to my terminal care working party and they also went to Cicely Saunders. We decided not to make a separate department for our dying patients in our hospital in Delft.

We officially started this palliative care in 1973 and we realised that even with the best palliative care you cannot stop all the suffering. I would suggest around 8 per cent. This is about the same group as in the hospices in England. In other words, you can stop pain in almost 95 per cent of all cases.

I was one of the first pain specialists in the Netherlands. I think I was the best at that time, so pain was not a reason for a patient to ask for euthanasia and it's still not the reason. In all our cases, only 5 per cent say that pain is the main reason why they ask for euthanasia. From then we realised we could not stop the suffering, even with the best palliative care available. When euthanasia was agreed it was always the decision of the patient and a combination of two doctors, the head nurse and nurses of that department. It also included one of our spiritual care-givers, at that time a Roman Catholic priest; later we had a humanistic one also. The decision was never mine. So if that group agreed we should do euthanasia, we would do it.

I did not do all the euthanasia cases myself. I think I have done on average five cases a year. Don't forget, it's an infrequent thing to do. In a normal GP practice the request for euthanasia is only once a year or once every two years. It's less than 2 per cent of all our dying cases. It's not a frequent thing. I have often laughed when doctors from other countries ask to come over and witness some cases of euthanasia, and I say there is no patient today or for the next three months.

Do you think in hospitals in England similar things are occurring as in Holland before the law was changed?

I discuss the practice with hospice doctors in England, some of whom think I am from Sodom and Gomorrah. We always come to the same conclusion, that we are both doing the same with terminal care and palliative care until the end. Then I am willing to stop life on the request of the patient, and British doctors will not. I am talking about the kind of patient who, if you do nothing, will literally suffocate. For instance, with cancer of the throat you can do many things – stomach tube, tracheotomy – but in the end the patient will suffocate. I ask the English, 'Why are you letting the patient suffocate?' They are good doctors, so what they do is give an overdose of sleeping pills or pain treatment so the patient will be unconscious, and then he will suffocate in that induced coma. I always then say, 'What's the difference?' The difference in my opinion is hypocrisy and is semantic. 'No,' they say, 'the difference is that you are doing something knowing that the patient will die for sure, and we do not have that intention.'

The law of murder is defined by intention and that's the difference.

What is the difference between turning off a ventilator and euthanasia? I know that the moment a ventilator is turned off the patient will die, so what's the difference? It is my intention that the patient will die and his suffering will come to an end. It is my intention, my right and my duty to stop the suffering of a patient who has unbearable suffering.

The difference, some might say, is that a respirator is taking on a function normally performed by an organ of the human body and in doing so is keeping the body alive. You take that away and the body dies. Euthanasia is an act where a substance is introduced with the specific intention of shortening the life of the patient.

You think it's different? In an emotional way, maybe. But what are medical ethics, who is defining medical ethics, and who has the authority to say what is ethical and what is not?

For centuries the Hippocratic Oath acted as a reference point. It defined medical practice and the boundaries of it.

Ethics are changing every year and every day. We are confronted today with ethical problems we have never thought about before. We've never thought about the possibility of manipulating genes or having a pregnant sixty-five-year-old. There are so many other things that have their own ethical problems, and we are solving them in our Western society with our Western ethics based on Western culture and nothing more.

You can go with the same problem to another culture, and you will find another ethical answer given by the same intelligent people who say they are the ethical thinkers of that society, but the outcome is completely different. For example, an Islamic ethicist or a Hindu will think completely differently over a lot of questions we think we have the right answer to.

Dr Peter Admiraal

In terms of your own personal ethics, why do you accept voluntary euthanasia and yet will not accept involuntary euthanasia?

Involuntary euthanasia is murder. That's how simple it is. I don't see any difference between murder and involuntary euthanasia. But you have to define what you mean by involuntary. In my opinion it is murder. But there may be circumstances where the patient didn't ask for euthanasia, but he is in an unbearable suffering position and he cannot ask for it because he is in a kind of coma. Is it then possible for a doctor to do euthanasia, in accordance with the family and with other doctors and nurses? This is non-voluntary euthanasia.

We have the famous 1,000 or 900 cases a year reported in the Remmelink Report of individuals who have been assisted to die with no specific request from the patient. I have done it myself, and I can give you a good example. There is a lung cancer patient who has no reason at all to ask for euthanasia, he is just dying from lung cancer. Sometimes that dying can be very prolonged and very upsetting for both the patient and his family. Sometimes patients in that terminal phase of lung cancer can lie there for two to four nights gasping for air. It is hard for the family, and they come to me and say, 'Is this the way he has to die?' and I tell them it's not the way he has to die, but he did not ask for euthanasia.

If that patient is in a coma there is no awareness, so he does not suffer, we think. There is never 100 per cent proof, though, and if I see these patients not only struggling for air but acting in the way that you and I would act when we are aware of pain, it is then I think I have to stop that suffering of both the patient and the family and stop this senseless struggling to die. I think most of the 900 patients referred to are in this category. A few hundred have earlier expressed their wish for euthanasia but have not confirmed it just before. They were all in a terminal phase of a disease and in the opinions of the doctors and nurses and their families, they were all suffering. Involuntary is murder and non-voluntary is without the request of the patient before he goes into a coma. I think there is a place for non-voluntary euthanasia. I have done it.

The example of lung cancer is a powerful case, where you have a patient who is breathless, is in a lot of pain and has a matter of hours to live. What about the severe geriatric case, a patient who is incontinent, not making any sense, who's staring at the ceiling a lot, with apparently no quality of life? Is this a situation where, if the relatives were saying, 'Dr Admiraal, he could go on for weeks and months like this,' you would practise euthanasia?

That's not a normal practice. Normally this patient will simply die because he doesn't eat and drink. If you stop keeping them alive they will die in a natural way. This is the reason we have hardly any active euthanasia in our nursing homes, because they simply die in a natural way. If you voluntarily stop eating you can survive for a month or three. If you stop drinking too you can last for about fourteen days. It's still very upsetting, it's complicated euthanasia or assisted suicide in my opinion, but you can do so. If you are dying in a natural way there is no reason to drink or to eat and you have no thirst. Doctors and nurses and family members often think this person must be thirsty and try and make them drink. In hospitals, not nursing homes, a good specialist will order an infusion of one or two litres a day, so they will keep you alive as long as the infusion runs. In nursing homes they have learned to go on with this kind of dying and they simply will not give water and food, and patients will die in the natural way. They have learned that you don't interfere with the normal dying process. But you can prolong the process by giving food and water.

Can I mention the current position in Australia? There they have translated a recent questionnaire into English and they are practising non-voluntary euthanasia about three times more than in the Netherlands. So it's much worse than in the Netherlands. However, we are open about it and I hope the same will be undertaken in Germany. I have always said, please do it in England. I'm so sure you will be astonished by the results if they fill in their questionnaires accurately. You will be astonished about what's going on. I think it's normal medical practice. Consider if you were terminally ill, in pain and suffering unbearably, having lost dignity and not able to make up your own mind. There are two doctors: one is going on with treatment but keeping you alive as long as possible, while the other one is saying, 'I will do my best to make your suffering as short as possible.' Which one would you choose?

In England we would say the question is irrelevant. The principle of double effect enables doctors to increase the dosage of morphine with the foreseen but unintended effect of shortening life, and unlike the Netherlands we have a hospice system which covers the whole of the UK so euthanasia is unnecessary.

Those English doctors are lying. The Netherlands has shown that with the best palliative care that statement is not true. There is palliative care in the Netherlands. I once quoted Cecily Saunders, who said that they have to pray and the Lord will help them. She is a very strong believer and believes your life is in God's hands. I respect her for that opinion but it's very far from my own opinion. I am a non-believer. It's nothing to do with the so-called God who has created the world and has our lives in his hands. I don't believe that. So you can see the difference between a religious ethical advisor and a non-religious ethical advisor. You can see how religion dominates ethics.

When the House of Lords Ethics Committee considered the matter, religion did not dominate it. What dominated the argument was that you couldn't create a law which would successfully protect all members of society from potential abuse.

The majority of anti-euthanasia groups have never seen a dying patient or been through the sorrows of a dying patient. How can you make your mind up if you have never seen one? If there are to be committees, they can be pro- and anti-euthanasia, but they always have to consist of doctors and nurses who are daily confronted with dying patients. That's fair. Later you can ask legal parties and ethicists and all the others, but in the beginning you should ask people who know the problems. None of the House of Lords Committee had been confronted with dying patients.

When certain medical groups gave evidence they said that Holland is a classic example of why we cannot have euthanasia, because Holland shows you can have a slide to non-voluntary euthanasia.

For twenty-five years we have been doing euthanasia in the Netherlands. There is no argument for the slippery slope, and no proof at all. I know you will say the proof is that we are doing euthanasia on severely handicapped newborn babies. It's involuntary, it's murder. It could be an argument of yours and I say yes, you are right. But it's not euthanasia because it's non-voluntary, and that's not murder in my opinion. On the other hand, if you see the arguments of the paediatricians doing this in about five to ten cases a year out of 30,000 or so babies, it's a tiny fraction. These babies are born, they are not breathing, there are a lot of defects, so they go to a neurological centre and they are checked. Their parents are informed of what's going on and if these groups say there is no possibility of doing anything then the baby goes back to the hospital. The air is disconnected, the baby is given to the mother and it dies in her arms. That's normal practice in your country as well. There are babies, a very few, who start respiration, who will die within a few weeks or months, but they are suffering. Experts can see that even these handicapped newborns are suffering, and it is now accepted in the Netherlands that in these very exceptional cases you can stop the lives by euthanasia. If you say this is proof of a slippery slope, that's up to you, but for me it's normal medical treatment and I think it's one of the blessings we have in this world that we can stop the suffering of these babies.

What about the Chabot case? The patient was suffering from depression, which most people in England would not see as unbearable suffering, as it can be treated.

It was not depression: she could have suffered for a longer time. That's what is important. Would you want to have responsibility for that? I have a simple answer to the question, 'Is it right for a doctor to stop the life of an unbearably suffering patient?' I can make it the reverse question: 'Is it right for you as a doctor to let a patient suffer as long as nature will, against his request?' Is that what you want?

A patient who asks me to stop his life goes through a lot of thinking. He never just says, 'I have cancer and I want to die.' My answer is always the same if that happens: I say, 'No, never at this moment.' All these patients from England, America, Germany, write me hundreds of letters asking to come over with their cancer. I always say, 'Stay in your country and try to find somebody who's caring for you. Realise the possibility that the chances you will die with euthanasia as a cancer patient will be less than 10 per cent, as in the Netherlands. Try to find somebody who cares for you. In your hospices they are caring for patients, it's one of the best institutions there is.'

What Cecily Saunders has done is the best you could do, recognising that with proper care, palliative care, you can care for a human being and you can cope with the suffering as far as possible. That's her message. But we say that if the patient accepts this care but says that their suffering is unacceptable for them as an individual, then, in my opinion, he has the right to ask me to stop his life. I have the right to refuse, to say, 'Never,' but I also have the right as a doctor to say, 'OK, if you want it then I can help you, but you must give me the opportunity to check your reasons.' That means I will never take the decision alone. I will ask another colleague, nurses, the pastor, and if we all agree that we cannot stop your suffering then we can proceed.

If you come to me with unbearable suffering, I could say, 'Oh no, your suffering is bearable.' That's a ridiculous attitude for a doctor. I can try to make the suffering bearable again, and that's what we do for all the patients who ask for euthanasia. We think over what we are doing wrong, what's to be improved, medication or the nursing care, what are we missing? If we all agree there is nothing more we can do and the patient says, 'I really want to die,' what other reasons, apart from religious reasons, are there that we should not do it?

Don't speak about ethics, don't speak about that. Consider 1850, 1900, 1950, 2000, 2050. We can mark each point in history with items like religion, sexuality, politics, discrimination, and there are more. You agree immediately that ethical definitions in 1850 are completely different from 1900, and completely different from 1950 and even more different now. Do you realise in 2050 they will laugh about our ethics and they will think that we are far away and happily gone!

There will be new ethics as there were in 1900, regarding 1850 as they are now regarding 1950. Can you compare today's views on religion or sexuality with 1950? It's only fifty years ago, so that means ethical problems will change and people will change their minds depending on the time they are living and what society says. If you go to India with our ethical problems, you will realise that their answers will be different from ours. Our ethical views are those of 1998 and they will not be the ideals of 2050. In 2050, 55 per cent of the population will be older than sixty-five. If this goes on, and I have no reason to doubt it, then the generation of 2050 will find themselves confronted with such unbelievable problems that they will find their own solutions.

Let me give you one example. We accept that an Alzheimer's patient is sometimes completely dependent on nursing care for, say, five to ten years. We accept caring for them and keeping them alive with artificial feeding. What will society think about these patients in the next fifty years? Maybe there will be an attitude that says this is completely senseless – as it is, in my opinion. My mother was completely demented for six years. She didn't recognise me, and that was completely senseless, in my opinion. As a non-religious man that was completely senseless. There was no reason to stop her life because in my opinion she was not suffering. In my opinion an Alzheimer's patient cannot suffer because he has no prospective thinking and no retrospective thinking. Maybe there will come a time when society says this costs money, we have not the money to keep them alive, so if they are demented for one year we will kill them. This could be the development.

You said first of all that you accepted psychiatric suffering, as in the Chabot case, as grounds for euthanasia. You said that with your mother you could see a case for euthanasia.

If you want to have some influence on the thinking of the next generation you have to control it now. You have to lay down very good rules. Maybe they can learn from what we have done. If you think that we in Holland have chosen the way of Sodom and Gomorrah you can think that, but you will witness that euthanasia will become acceptable.

Do you see it as an answer to an ageing population?

No, I see it as an answer to unbearable suffering, to the fact that you don't have to accept you will die with unbearable suffering. I see it as an answer on self-determination, determination, one of the most humanistic principles there is. I am a humanist, a member of the International Academy of Humanists, and we think self-determination is the most principal right we have. I have great respect for others and their wishes, but it is up to me how to make the decisions. Maybe we are all living in Sodom and Gomorrah and we are poisoned by the idea of euthanasia; I don't know.

You should recall Dutch medical experience and the five years of occupation under the Nazis, who tried to introduce involuntary euthanasia in the Netherlands as well. There was a strike by all doctors and nurses, and several hundred were sent to concentration camps. We still refused to accept the German euthanasia law in the Netherlands.

You can accuse us of forgetting very quickly and of being a rotten society, and I have to live with that. Some might see it as a kind of virus spread around our doctors. About 50 per cent of our doctors have done euthanasia at least once. Thirty-five per cent are willing to do it under some circumstances but, as I said, in general practice this request is made very seldom. The remaining group of around 15 per cent will not help you themselves but they are willing to send you to another doctor, and only 2 per cent of all our doctors in the Netherlands are not willing to help you and not willing to send you to another doctor.

Our biggest anti-euthanasia and abortion society has only 2 per cent membership of doctors, and every year it is less. Maybe we are infected with a kind of death fear. It is up to you, but I think we are living in a very open society where we have respect for others and respect for self-determination, and we accept that patients can ask to stop their lives. Of course, you have a duty to make that number as small as possible by giving them the best palliative care there is. That's one of the best things Cecily Saunders has brought. But then you will see that you cannot stop the request for euthanasia 100 per cent.

You can deny it, but we know better. I remember visiting Cicely Saunders in 1968 with a new morphine-type drug you could take by mouth, which was brand new at that time. She was not interested at all, so they did not use it and it was only used in Belgium and the Netherlands. Cecily Saunders was giving her patients a drink six times a day, a cocktail consisting of morphine, heroin, some alcohol and a tranquilliser. They also got a mixture of sleeping pills and sedatives. So they got a mixture of six different drugs every four hours.

We Dutch doctors were astonished as these patients were like zombies. You can have proper treatment without interfering with your mind and remain quite alert and normal. I don't know what they are doing today, but if you take care of patients the way they do in hospices, it's the best there is. I have always advocated that there should be no euthanasia without palliative care. Euthanasia can only be the last dignified act of palliative care, but they don't want to listen and say that here in the Netherlands we are giving euthanasia instead of treatment and because we have no palliative care. That is a lie.

Of course we can improve palliative care. We might not have hospice buildings but are giving the same palliative care as you in our hospitals. As a result people say we are doing euthanasia because we have no hospices. Sometimes I think I am old enough and intelligent enough to stop all this because I know what is going on in the Netherlands. I was in Germany last month and at the end of my lecture there was a Catholic priest who said, 'I know the truth!'; he had read a journal that said 40 per cent of our handicapped people are killed. It's the biggest lie ever. We are keeping alive all our handicapped patients the best way in the world. There has never been a handicapped patient given euthanasia. Maybe our 2 per cent of opponents are telling lies about what is going on.

Cardinal Winning

Biographical details

Cardinal Winning has been the Catholic Archbishop of
Glasgow since 1974. Prior to that he was a parish priest in
Motherwell and Clydebank.

The Cardinal has been President of the Bishops' Conference of Scotland since 1985 and takes a keen and active
interest in ethical concerns. In particular he has been an
ardent critic of the current abortion law and has spoken on
the issue many times in the national media.

Introductory comments

The Church has played a significant role in the public policy
debates surrounding euthanasia in both the United States and
Australia. In this country a number of senior clerics have
played an increasingly important role. The former Archbishop of York, Lord Habgood, was a member of the House
of Lords Select Committee which considered the matter, and
both Cardinal Hume and Cardinal Winning have written and
spoken publicly on the issue. An interview with the Archbishop of Canterbury was requested for this publication but
was declined.

The Church teaches that human life is a gift from
God which is to be preserved and cherished. Every

individual possesses intrinsic value and worth, irrespective of their mental state or their physical condition. A person's dignity is not measured by mental capacity or physical circumstances. The dignity is assured by their humanity rather than by any subjective definition of personhood or quality-of-life indicators. Euthanasia is morally unacceptable to the Church, for it requires a judgment that an individual's life is no longer worth living. Both the Catholic and the Protestant Church believe that euthanasia is not compatible with the Christian faith and should not be permitted in civil legislation.

Despite this overriding principle of the sanctity of life, the Church does not perceive that it is incompatible with the appropriate withdrawal of medical treatment. The Church believes that doctors do not have an overriding obligation to prolong life by all possible means. Death is an inevitable consequence of life, and doctors are obliged to provide appropriate treatment rather than every treatment that is technically possible. When assessing questions of treatment, the Church believes that the treatment should be proportionate to the therapeutic benefit expected and should never be disproportionately burdensome or futile, so that it would not have the desired physiological effect.

The Churches expressed varying degrees of concern over the Bland verdict and Cardinal Winning explores this further in the interview. The Cardinal shares the view of others in this book that while it is appropriate to withdraw medical treatment where it will be of no further benefit to the patient, the withdrawal of nutrition and hydration is unacceptable medical practice. There is a difference between the withdrawal of a life-support machine which is undertaking a function on behalf of a failing organ in the body and the withdrawal of food and fluid, the means by which we all survive. The Cardinal finds the Bland case unacceptable medical practice.

Other Churches and clerics share his view with varying degrees of enthusiasm.

Interview

I would be grateful if you would outline the position of the Catholic Church with regard to euthanasia in general.

The Catholic Church's attitude to euthanasia is that it is very gravely wrong. The definition of euthanasia in the Church would be an action, either something positive or an omission, which of itself or by intention causes death, with the aim that suffering will thereby be avoided. In other words, you can carry out euthanasia just by omitting to do something you really ought to do. One of the flaws in the suggested reforms by the Lord Chancellor is that euthanasia is seen as a deliberate act, a positive intervention, and we maintain that the definition is not large enough to include an act of omission. You could do nothing, somebody is near death and you could do nothing. You could withhold feeding and liquids and just sit back and wait for death to take place. We felt that by using this very narrow definition they were excluding the possibility that voluntary euthanasia could take place just by doing nothing.

Would you consider there are times when it is appropriate to withdraw treatment?

Yes, but I don't want to anticipate that. What we are saying is that we regard food and drink as human rights. To deny those is to deny human rights, and therefore it would be against the law. Very often in today's society and today's legal discussions food and drink is regarded as medical treatment, but it's not, it's quite different to medical treatment.

The next question after defining euthanasia would be: why is euthanasia wrong? Why is it wrong to bring about the death of somebody else, just to avoid pain? In any civilised society there must be basic law that shows respect for all human life. That's not based on church teaching, but it's based on natural law. Human life is invaluable, innocent human life is inviolable and the only time the state can take human life is to right an injustice – in other words when somebody's committed a crime where the punishment is death.

The other question is why is there so much talk about euthanasia nowadays, and the reason is there are so many cultural changes. First of all, human life is cheap today as a result of various laws that have been passed. For example, from our abortion law 500 unborn children die per day in the UK. There is a weakening of the basic traditional values with regard to human life and it's very paradoxical that at the same time and the same area of the world where people's unborn children are being eliminated there is a strong campaign against capital punishment. Other cultural changes have arisen from the medical advances. People are living a lot longer and decisions about ending life are being made where before they didn't arise at all because people died. In the Victorian age, dying at forty years of age or so was fairly common. Now people can go on to be a hundred, and very many people live into their mid-eighties or even nineties. There is a deterioration – if you look at someone who's ninety years of age very often there's a great deterioration – not to mention the growth of Alzheimer's disease, senility and degenerative conditions. I think if you didn't have any faith and you didn't believe in an after-life it would be fairly understandable that people would say, 'I want to finish it off before I suffer too much.'

Can I come back to the point about food and water? The House of Lords Select Committee in 1992/93 came up with this position where providing food and water through artificial means was to be seen as medical treatment and spoon-feeding was to be seen as nursing care, the significance being that if a treatment is of no benefit to the patient you can withdraw medical treatment, which I think we would all agree with in general principle.

The Catholic Church would teach that, too. When it's a question of how much treatment you should give a person and when you should stop it, there are various components to look at. Is it very difficult, is there a big risk involved, is it proportionate to the condition of the person, and what's the cost? For example, giving someone chemotherapy when they are in extremis would be regarded as out of all proportion to the benefit that would accrue.

But some members of the medical profession will argue that the provision of food and water involving an operation to place a gastrostomy into somebody's stomach is medical treatment. It involves a medical procedure to begin it and to withdraw it and clean it up. There's no way you can describe it as care. What would you say to that argument?

It depends on how you define medical treatment. It doesn't need to be medicine. I would look on medical treatment as something that has to do with medicine. This includes nutrition. Fifty years ago there may not have been nutritional drips for very ill people, but they exist here today and therefore they should be used if they are not too burdensome to the patient. Some people would say that in a condition such as where the person has just been through a big operation and there is not any hope of recovery, to begin that kind of drip-feeding might well be pointless. But if you have begun it, it's quite wrong to withdraw it afterwards. There's a major distinction between allowing dying patients to die, for example to die with dignity, without making any futile attempts to keep them alive, and forcing doctors and nurses to dehydrate and starve a patient to death. For humane reasons alone the feeding by artificial means would be demanded, but if your doctor is saying to make that happen you have got to put this man through extensive surgery which he is not capable of sustaining, it would be a question they have to think about.

One of the things about the Bland judgment was this. There is a view that the youngster was kept alive to make him a test case. I have talked to experts about this and they have said it's practically certain that in the period of time he was in a coma there must have been at least two or three occasions when he would have contracted pneumonia and they would have given him antibiotics. To give someone antibiotics in a vegetative state, with no prospect of recovery, was extraordinary and, one would say, unnecessary. Perhaps he could have been left to die on several occasions.

Will the Bland judgement have strengthened the call for euthanasia?

There are plenty of pressure groups who advocate euthanasia. They have been in existence for forty or fifty years and we have to make this distinction between their present objectives and their ultimate aspirations. Their present objective is to encourage people to assume an attitude where they would want to ask doctors, 'Don't let me live if I'm in difficulty and I'm sick.' That would be voluntary euthanasia. The way they want to reach direct euthanasia is through voluntary euthanasia, gradually changing the attitudes of people to want to die with fairly reasonable cause. 'I do not want to suffer too much, don't give me the treatment.' 'Let's just let that person die, let's give them a lethal dose.' That happens already, and it's quite amazing, the large number of doctors who are in these euthanasia groups.

What the government and probably the Lord Chancellor said to you recently was, 'We have no desire to change the law with regard to euthanasia. We are against euthanasia; the Bland judgment was not euthanasia in our minds.' But you are on a completely different ethical track from the government and they don't appear to want to listen to this point.

They don't need to change the law on euthanasia. Living wills and the legally binding advance directives are such that I can write an advance directive saying, 'I don't want any medical treatment, I want the feeding to be withdrawn, I don't want any liquids. I want to go as quickly as possible.' If somebody wants to do that, let them do it themselves, I would say. But to oblige someone else to do it, against his professional integrity and against his conscience, is wrong.

The situation with regard to abortions today in Great Britain is that there is practically no Catholic gynaecologist left in the whole system. The consultant we had in a recent meeting with the Lord Chancellor made that point. It's very easy to say, as one of our MPs said, who's also a surgeon, 'It's not the time to change the law on euthanasia.' You don't need to, because if the Bland judgment becomes statutory all they need to do is to stand back and watch the person die. They can withhold treatment and feeding, but at the moment it's got to go to the High Court. The medical profession is not quite sure of itself with regard to PVS. For example, the recent case of the young lady in Bournemouth caused controversy. After she had been in a coma for months and months the doctors decided to cut off her food, which they did. They then cut off the fluids and were about to remove the tube when her mother asked her to blink her eyes if she understood, and she did. Now she's doing a university degree and is about to sue the hospital.

Part of the Lord Chancellor's Mental Incapacity Report which you have reservations about refers to advance directives. What is your fear about advance directives? Why can't people write down in advance what they would or would not like? Surely you are depriving people of their autonomy and their own personal choice?

First of all, there is a new concept coming into the law in the UK. Previously, if you study the common law and also the European Convention on Human Rights, you will see that the inviolability of human life was paramount in the common law. There is a new concept which is being introduced which is competing with that inviolability for supremacy, and that's personal autonomy or self-determination.

That means people can decide what they want to do with their own life. We are trying to show that personal autonomy is, of its very nature in society, limited. For example, the law on seat belts, or the criminalisation of people who possess drugs.

Why can't I say in an advance directive that if I am in a car accident and go into PVS I don't wish to be fed?

The advance directive is all right. If you want to commit suicide, go ahead and do it. To oblige someone else, though, perhaps against their conscience, and to make it unlawful for them to refuse to do what you want, I think it's quite irrational and immoral.

Do you think advance directives are being used as a tool to introduce euthanasia, and if so, how are they going to do that?

I think the euthanasia lobby is promoting advance directives because that is the way to promote the attitude in society that people can take their own lives. It sounds very reasonable: 'I don't want to suffer and don't give me any treatment.' But to bind somebody else to fulfil that for you is quite wrong.

You mention autonomy and this new legal attitude that's embracing the healthcare professions, self-determination. Some doctors now believe that it is best to define humanity by one's ability to think rationally, to make decisions and to make perfect choices. Human life should be afforded the utmost respect, but the changes in medical science have forced us to rethink how we define it. What do you say to that definition?

First, who would decide whose life is worth living? And second, it's an old definition, not new at all. It's old in the sense that these euthanasia groups have been plugging away at this for years. One British physician wrote thirty years ago regarding the aged and the senile that decisions regarding the senile would have to be taken within the next twenty years. He said something like: the number of old people is increasing by leaps and bounds. Pneumonia, the old man's friend, is now checked by antibiotics. Effects of hardship, exposure, starvation and accident are now minimised. Where is this leading us? What of the drooling helpless disorientated old man, or the incontinent old woman lying in a bed? Is it here that the need for euthanasia exists? Now?

Do you find the definition demeaning to humanity or is it treating humanity with respect?

This definition of what is humanity is a purely arbitrary one. For example, up to the mid 1980s no one had ever used the term 'pre-embryo'. The Warnock Commission had to get round it and make it possible for experts to experiment on the human embryo. They were not allowed to do it, so they coined this term, 'pre-embryo', which said that for the first fourteen days of that embryo's life it is not an individual and therefore we can experiment on it. That's what they are doing now.

Do you think the 'right to die' language is helpful to the debate?

That's sheer manipulation of words, just as happened in the embryo debate. What we described as human life in that debate they chose to call 'potential' human life.

Pro-euthanasia campaigners say it's not the quantity of life but the quality of life that matters. Would you agree?

I'm interested in the quality of life as well, but it's nothing to do with quantity. It's an individual. They have a right to life, no matter what the quality. Who's to decide what the quality of life is, Ludovic Kennedy?

They say it's voluntary and they have a right to death as well as a right to life.

As far as I'm concerned, if they want to commit suicide, let them do it, it's no longer a criminal offence, but as far as obliging other people to assist them in that, that is still a criminal offence in the United Kingdom, and if these proposals become statutory it will no longer be a criminal offence.

If it was changed, how would it affect our society?

It would be very radical. First of all, when you go to hospital you look on a nurse as an angel of healing and mercy and the doctor as somebody who's going to heal you. The Hippocratic Oath says that in so many words. In ten years' time, if these proposals become law, people would no longer have an image of the doctor as a person of healing. There would be a change in the doctor–patient relationship which would contribute to what the Pope calls 'the culture of death'.

Can I quote from Joseph Fletcher's book, *Humanhood, Essays in Biomedical Ethics*, where he itemises the following characteristics, indicators of humanhood which must hold good if somebody is to be regarded as certainly a person:

He should have a minimum IQ of 40, he should be self-aware, be capable of exercising self-control, a sense of temporal duration, a sense of the future, a sense of the past, capable of entering into relationships, capable of concern for others, be in communication with others, be in control of his existence, be inquisitive, be capable of adapting to and initiating change in his own way of life. He should enjoy a balance of reason and emotion in his life. He should be idiosyncratic or distinctive. He should have a functioning cortex.

That would eliminate about 90 per cent of the human race. You can make as many qualifications as you like to narrow down humanhood to suit your purposes. That's just Nazism at its worst. It's developed Nazism.

In Holland 1,000 out of 3,000 euthanasia cases that have taken place did not make any explicit request to die.

I have been surprised, when discussing the issue with some in favour of euthanasia, that they see it as a religious battle, that the main enemy is the Catholic Church. Do you see that as the way this debate is going to move forward or do you see it in a different light?

They will always plant a label on it like that, and because Catholics don't always enjoy 100 per cent support in society, you rubbish the message by rubbishing the medium. I'm not surprised at that, but I want to emphasise that any civilised society must have as a basic law absolute respect for human life. It's a question of natural law, which the Church of England supports, the Church of Scotland supports, the Evangelicals support and the Jews support.

Do you see the debate as a medical issue?

It's disappointing that some medical experts are in the forefront of the euthanasia campaign because doctors, generally speaking, unless they have developed their ethical attitudes, have no great insight into ethical issues. They are medical and they would view ageing life as something that could be eliminated because it's past its best.

So you think the ethical training of doctors is inadequate in this country?

Absolutely. I know a couple of people who have been trying to establish some kind of basic principles dealing with the elderly and the senile. One of them is a professor of geriatrics in London and the other is a world theologian, a Catholic priest. They have been working together and interviewing students and nurses and doctors, and they are finding that people have good sentiments about things. They are trying to give them basic principles that don't originate from the Roman Catholic Church but are accepted by the Church – in other words, the moral law principles. For example, you don't have to go to religion to find out the best interests of a sick old person. One of the things not in their best interest is to kill them. The best interest is to treat them with loving care until they die, and if society is not prepared to do that then there's something wrong with society. Someone like Ludovic Kennedy would disagree with that even if it was his mother – I think she did leave some kind of directive like that. The argument they have against palliative care and the hospice movement is that there is not enough to go round. I have spoken to people who run hospices and they tell me there is no reason why anybody dying today should die in pain.

Looking to the future, are you quite pessimistic about where this debate is going or do you think in the long term the views that you are espousing will hold fast?

I'm pessimistic about society and the values of society today, certainly. But reading between the lines and considering what the Lord Chancellor said the other day, that he shared our concerns, I would hope that at least some of these proposals which seem to be particularly horrific will never become law. We have not discussed the subject that the incapacitated should become subject to experiments, provided these experiments did not harm them significantly. I think that pretty awful, to experiment on them if they can't give their consent. A lot of these people will have no dependants. Does that mean we go to the most vulnerable in our society and use them as objects of experimentation?

One very strong point. The number of MPs who fought to ban fox hunting didn't have a clue about the Lord Chancellor's document *Who Decides*? It's quite extraordinary that they worry about animal experimentation and fox hunting, and there are 500 unborn babies dead every day in Britain. There is a medical establishment in Edinburgh which wants to produce embryos and experiment on them because they can take out this tissue from the brain of the unborn and use it cure Parkinson's disease and diabetes and HIV. To a person who has not thought about it that's of benefit to the human race. To cure Parkinson's disease is a wonderful thing, but the end doesn't justify the means. That's only one other example of the cheapness of human life. They can produce life in a test-tube and then use it as they like.

Sir Ludovic Kennedy

Biographical details

Ludovic Kennedy has enjoyed a highly successful career as a writer and broadcaster. He has written as a columnist for many publications including *Newsweek* and the *Spectator* and has presented and introduced numerous television programmes.

A longstanding member of the Liberal Party, he stood on a number of occasions as the Liberal candidate in Rochdale.

Ludovic Kennedy is currently President of the Voluntary Euthanasia Society and spends considerable time speaking on the matter. He has written a book on the issue, entitled *Euthanasia and the Good Death*.

Introductory comments

A focus of many arguments in favour of euthanasia is the principle of personal autonomy which finds expression in the language of rights and choice. Recently, as people have gained a greater degree of control in every area of their lives, this has added strength to those who wish to control the final scenes of their life.

This new mood for personal autonomy finds support in the healthcare professions. Both the medical and nursing professions are committed to respecting the

155

principle of patient autonomy and to seeking out the views of their patients. While there are undoubtedly health-care professionals who retain a more paternalistic out-look, the new direction of the professions is clearly visible.

The support for patient autonomy has been assisted by the rapid advances in medical science. While such advances have brought great benefits to many, more people are facing degenerative conditions than ever before. The prospect of a lengthy decline, or worse still of having a life artificially prolonged, has intensified the calls for euthanasia.

At the same time, those in the euthanasia movement have questioned the relevance of the sanctity of human life. They believe that it is based on religious sentiments which have less support today, and that the present-day consensus would be more accurately reflected by the phrase 'respect for life'.

Adhering strongly to the concept of patient autonomy, the pro-euthanasia movement has promoted advance directives as a solution to some of the practical problems associated with recording a patient's wishes. In particular, they enable doctors to be aware of the wishes of individuals should a patient become incompetent.

Advance directives, or living wills, as they are known, have been prevalent in America for a number of years. With the passing of the People's Self-Determination Act and a more aggressive type of healthcare, such documents are becoming increasingly popular in the United States.

In Britain they have been heavily promoted by the Volunt-ary Euthanasia Society who have drafted their own directive. Following the House of Lords Select Committee on Medical Ethics, the BMA produced a booklet offering guidelines on the use of advance directives by healthcare practitioners in the UK. Despite this helpful publication, there remains some confusion as to how far doctors should abide by wishes as expressed in advance directives. Some believe that there is a reasonable body of common law which effectively renders them legally binding on a doctor. Others believe that comments surrounding the use of advance directives in the Bland judgment and other cases are comments on issues of concern rather than statements of the current law.

The interview covers these issues in some detail. In the course of the discussion Ludovic Kennedy makes the case that doctors are committing euthanasia in this country but are afraid to admit it. He describes the principle of double effect as a 'loophole' and dishonest, and calls passionately for a change in law.

Interview

Let us begin with Lord Irvine's Mental Incapacity Report, published by the government to consider decision-making for those who are not able to make decisions for themselves. The report focuses on the issue of advance directives. The VES and the 'right to die' groups around the world seem to promote them heavily; why do you think they do that? What is in the advance directive that they are so keen on?

Their appeal is that if you are rendered incompetent, what Lord Irvine refers to as 'without capacity', when you can no longer look after your own affairs, you are saving a lot of people time and worry and maybe expense in having people look after you. I am talking about people in PVS; not people in a temporary coma who may then recover, but people like Tony Bland who, as you know, was non-competent for three or four years. Since you have become no use to man nor beast nor yourself, there is no need for other people to look after you. That's the basic thing about them.

*So you would not see them just applying to people in PVS;
their use will be much wider. One of the things causing
controversy is the issue of food and fluid and whether
or not you can ask for the withdrawal of nutrition and
hydration. Do you think advance directives should be able
to do that?*

Yes, I do.

*You don't think food and fluid are a basic human right which
should not be withdrawn from patients?*

Just tell me what the point of that is. What is the point of
keeping alive somebody who is in PVS and is never going
to be anything else? You've got to be certain about
their condition, but having become certain it seems to be
absolutely pointless. From my point of view, I would not
wish my wife or daughter or anybody else to be kept alive
as a living vegetable. If that happened to me I think it would
be quite obscene as well as a terribly selfish thing to
demand.

*But by advocating that, surely you are advocating people
dying in a terrible way? They may not know anything about
it, but starvation is a distressing way to die, taking about
thirteen or fourteen days.*

If you are so far gone that you are not aware of it happening it cannot be a terrible death. Maybe it would be quicker
and kinder to give the person an injection, but that is
a deliberate act of killing which I think is perfectly
acceptable as long as it's voluntary. But it must be voluntary
– that is, if you are in your right mind. If you are not in

your right mind it's neither here nor there.

One of the Law Lords in the Bland judgment stated that they were being asked if it was permissible to shorten the life of the patient. There is no difference in the Bland judgment between on the one hand actively killing him with barbiturates and on the other hand actually shortening his life by taking away his food and water.

It's not quite the same thing. I think from a moral point of view a lot of people would go along with what I am saying, but if you said, 'Give him a lethal injection,' it might, for illogical reasons, meet opposition.

I can understand people saying, 'Let him just fade away, but don't actually take a violent action to end his life.' It's all to do with quality of life; that's what we care about in the VES, not the length of life but the quality. We're all going to die some time. As long as you've got a quality of life, life is worth living. If the quality is gone then there's not much point.

Was the Bland judgment euthanasia?

I don't think it much matters what you call it. I think the important thing is to make it acceptable. You can call it anything you like. Some people might call it passive euthanasia, which is a pejorative phrase, but I don't see it like that at all. I think we have got to get used to the idea. By the year 2030 more than half the population of Europe will be over sixty – that's quite a thought – so the pressures will continue to grow. We are going to have to accept the fact that the length of life is not what matters, it's the quality.

On the issue of advance directives, you mention that the primary use you saw was for those in PVS. But PVS only concerns about 2,000 people at the most in the UK, a very small minority. Motor neurone disease, severe geriatric conditions, Alzheimer's, the degenerative diseases of the latter part of the twentieth century, are as I understand it a much greater proportion. Do you think that it is acceptable for someone who is an Alzheimer's sufferer to be able to refuse nutrition and hydration via a tube to the nose or the stomach, in the form of an advance directive?

If you become non-competent and you have signed a declaration, which I have done, deposited with your doctor stating that if you do get into such a condition you do not wish to be kept artificially alive, that's all right.

And by 'artificially alive' you would mean also food and water?

Yes. That's what happened to Tony Bland, as you know.

I think it was one of the neurologists who said that Bland's brain was a vacuous state, there was nothing there at all. I would have thought that in an Alzheimer's victim or someone with a degenerative disorder, that moment of withdrawing nutrition and hydration might come much sooner, while they are still competent. What I am interested in knowing is if you feel that withdrawing food and fluid, is OK with those types of conditions as well as with PVS. In a few years' time, will we see a growing number of people moving on to another place as a result of not having food and

160

water? Would you see that as being the case?

I disagree about 'moving on to another place' – what place? Apart from that I would say yes, spot on.

And therefore the pressure for euthanasia will intensify, will it not, because the nurses in the Bland judgment said that they were very upset by having to watch what happened.

Voluntary euthanasia, yes. Euthanasia without choice, no. I think it's a hurdle we've all got to get used to and overcome. It may sound to you a bit callous but it's the way many of us see it – as a major step forward in human affairs. In my view the sanctity of life is not absolute.

Can I mention one or two things that you said in your book? You state that the argument about life being sacred is non-sense and that what really matters is not the length of life but the quality of it. How on earth do you measure quality? In a sense the religious groups have an absolute. That might be easy, it might be an over-simplification, but they have a clear position. What indicators do you use?

If you are no longer competent you don't have any quality of life, it's not there to measure. And if you don't have a quality of life you don't have an enjoyment of life because there's nothing to actively enjoy.

How would you define competence?

In the simplest kind of way, by saying that you don't make sense any more, that you can't respond in a meaningful way to anything that anybody says to you – and, what is more, you never will.

If the quality of life is decided by whether or not an individual can think effectively for themselves, make decisions, act in an autonomous way, there are a lot of people in society who can't do that. Severely mentally handicapped people don't have the capacity to make choices, severe geriatrics don't have the capacity to make choices, and therefore I wonder, on the measurement that the VES and you use here, where those people stand within that quality of life definition.

It must be a medical decision. That is vital. It must be a medical decision. A doctor or doctors must make that decision. No awareness of life, that's the proper definition. No awareness of being anybody. No awareness of relationships. No awareness of anything.

Do you believe that in those circumstances we should be able to make a choice in advance regarding treatment decisions?

Yes, of course, and legally we can already.

Would you ever advocate that you or I should make a choice on behalf of an individual who is in that state?

That's a good question and it's come up before, but I think the voluntary issue is the important aspect. I have always thought that. You make an advance declaration saying what your wishes are in certain circumstances and these must be followed, and in common law now they have to be followed. I would like to see advance directives in every doctor's waiting room in the country, and a massive advertising campaign by the government informing everyone about them.

There seem to be many definitions of euthanasia, and for that reason the House of Lords called their Committee the Medical Ethics Committee. How would you personally define it?

As you know, the literal definition is 'the good death' from the Greek words *eu* and *thanatos*. But the word can be misleading. That's why in the VES we are thinking of changing the name – we are part of the Right to Die Association, which is a worldwide body – simply because of the emotional content of the word 'euthanasia' in many people's minds who associate it with Hitler and the gypsies, etc. They think it means putting somebody to death with or without their permission. The important thing is that it's voluntary, it must be requested, as in Holland.

The point about language is important, and therefore 'right to die' is a more effective way of describing what you are about.

It's more acceptable to most people, while 'euthanasia' is not. It's a fear that somebody's going to do something to you against your will. That's what's in many people's minds. That's Cecily Saunders' great cry: once you make it permissible, it's the thin end of the wedge, there will be no end to it and it will become involuntary quite soon. I just don't agree with that – why should it?

But the evidence from the Netherlands supports that. In the Remmelink Report in 1990 there were a thousand deaths where doctors admitted that euthanasia had occurred with no direct request.

You must get this right. This is the thing that all the anti-euthanasia groups bring up the whole time. What makes you think it doesn't happen here, and in other countries in the West? These doctors in Holland were being absolutely honest, as they were asked to be. Very often when a patient is within days or hours of death and is in some anguish and discomfort, the doctor knows he is within a short time of death. The relatives who are gathered round the bed will say to the doctor, 'Please could you do something to hurry this along, it's so awful having to watch this, for all of us.' It's awful for the doctor, too, and it is at that moment that he will give an extra dose of diamorphine. It happens here. You ask any doctor and he will tell you that it happens.

There is no proof of what you are saying in terms of the UK. You say it happens here, but where is the evidence?

Go and ask doctors. If you are going to do a thorough survey of this subject, go and ask the medical profession who are prepared to be honest. It is a fact.

There are a number of cases where that has happened. The Cox case, for example, which you wrote on for the Daily Telegraph, *where he intentionally shortened the life of a patient. Are they practising the principle of double effect?*

Yes, if you give diamorphine. Dr Cox gave potassium chloride, the only effect of which is to kill. It has no beneficial effect at all and it just brought her life to an end. She had asked him a week earlier if he would bring her life to an end because she was suffering so much. He refused her then, but on this occasion she was howling like a dog, as one of the nurses said, and the situation was just getting too much for him. Something like potassium chloride does the job immediately, whereas diamorphine doesn't. People's metabolisms are quite different; a dose of diamorphine may shorten one person's life by perhaps a fortnight and with someone else it could be three months or three days. It's a very uncertain drug. If voluntary euthanasia became legal I would like to see a drug which would have a more immediate effect.

Doctors say they are not practising euthanasia, they are merely treating the pain. They are not killing the patient.

That is what they say, that's their loophole. They are able to say they are not killing the patient, they are relieving the pain, keeping the patient comfortable. It may be so and it may be not; you can't tell.

So what language would you use to describe that principle?

I would say it's a very easy way out for the medical profession, because nobody's going to say to a doctor, 'We don't think you were doing that only to ease his pain or suffering. We are thinking it's because you both felt it was time for him to go.'

We talked about the slide to involuntary euthanasia and you questioned that. You don't think that is what is happening in Holland; you think the law is working effectively. There was a case in 1994 called the Chabot case where a woman was suffering from psychiatric problems following a tragic series of events in her family. Two doctors claimed she was suffering from severe psychiatric depression and her life was shortened at her request. The doctor was pardoned. I just wondered whether you thought it was right for someone who is in that condition to be able to request euthanasia?

I take the point. Sometimes it's awfully difficult to separate depression, which can be temporary, from a genuine and sustained wish for life to be ended. I think you have got to trust the medical profession to know what they are doing. There are two or three cases in this country where doctors have done that sort of thing, and there's one doctor in Newcastle, who has been waiting for three or four months for the police to decide whether to prosecute him or not. So you can find exceptions to the rule wherever you look. I think I'm right in saying there's only been one prosecution in Holland of a doctor who did this without the patient's consent, and he was given a year's imprisonment.

The Dutch situation arose from the development of case law in the 1970s and 1980s. Doctors were pushing the boundaries of the law, which resulted in a change, later sanctioned although not legalised by the Parliament. Do you think that is the process we're in in Britain?

I think so, yes, I think it is.

Do you think that's orchestrated by the euthanasia and the 'right to die' lobby?

No, I don't. It springs from the grass roots. For a long time now public opinion polls have shown upwards of 80 per cent of people approving of the principle of voluntary euthanasia. The latest information from the British Medical Association is that there are now marginally more doctors in favour than against, more doctors who said if it was made legal they would be prepared, given adequate safeguards, to practise it. So the whole thing is gradually moving forward.

The House of Lords Committee unanimously rejected any suggestion of legalising euthanasia. Surely this was a step back for the euthanasia movement in the UK?

Yes, the House of Lords Committee was pretty weighted against us. Its Chairman, Lord Walton of Detchant, represented the old medical establishment, who certainly don't want any change. Lord McColl is another, then there's Peter Rawlinson who's a Roman Catholic, and the Archbishop of York. It was full of establishment figures. Yet Baroness Jay, who I know is in favour, didn't write a dissenting report, nor did Lady Llewelyn Davies, who was actually a member of the VES. Those two could have helped the whole movement forward but they chose not to.

When you listen to those who are against euthanasia, there are a number of arguments they put forward – the sanctity of life, the issue that it's impossible to police. What is the main reason for the need for a change in law? Is it that the current law is not working? Is it that medical practices have advanced? Is it the dignity issue? What convinced you of the need for euthanasia?

I will tell you exactly. My mother went in to a nursing home when she was eighty-two. I went to see her on one occasion and said, 'How are you today?' She said, 'Pretty mouldy. I can't read any more and I don't enjoy the television. I do listen to the radio, but that is all there is. I'm absolutely exhausted. I have had a wonderful life, I have enjoyed every minute of it. Now the time has come for it to end, but of course I can't end it.'

I was astonished, because it had never occurred to me that anybody, particularly my own mother, should actually want to die. She did want to and it had a great effect on me. I realised she couldn't be the only person in the world who felt like that; there must be others. The more I looked into it, the more I found there were hundreds and thousands of others, and that's what led me to the movement.

So it was very personal?

Yes, very much, but I also found it was a wish which was growing. In 1945 there was a poll taken showing the number of those in favour as under 50 per cent of those canvassed, and now in poll after poll and debate after debate it's 80–90 per cent. I have taken part in and won many university debates because nearly everybody present either has a relation or knows of a friend who has a relation whose quality of life has gone and who longs to die and can't.

You must not be afraid of death, you see. I think people were afraid of death in Victorian times, and certainly earlier. I don't believe anybody is afraid of death now, but I think they are terrified of dying. I know I am. A long drawn-out period of loss of dignity with only one end is what people want to avoid if they possibly can. I'm amazed at the resilience of the human race, when people are told, 'You have got cancer, and if you are lucky you have got a year or, if you are not so lucky, six months.' It's an extraordinary thing how people do adjust, but they do, they accept it. I have always been struck how prisoners condemned to execution have accepted the idea of their deaths. It's because they have to; it would be intolerable for them if they didn't.

One of the arguments against euthanasia is the fact that we live in a society and each individual's personal autonomy has to be balanced, yours with mine, in order for us to build up a society in which we can all live. Others state that legalising euthanasia will damage the medical profession and the success of hospice care. Some have suggested old people will feel pressurised into requesting euthanasia. All this because you wish to exercise your personal autonomy. Don't you feel your actions have to be balanced with the autonomy of others?

I don't think euthanasia will affect your autonomy at all.

If I live in fear as a result of doctors being able to practise it?

You won't live in fear. The people I have met in hospitals are not afraid that if it was legalised they might be put away before their time. Their fear is that permission to be granted won't come in time.

On the actual changes in law there are a number of possibilities: a new Act of mercy killing, the legalisation of advance directives, the legalisation of euthanasia per se, *or a situation similar to Holland whereby it goes to a prosecutor to investigate after the doctor has informed. What do you think would be the ideal legal solution?*

It should no longer be a crime for a doctor to help a person to die who has repeatedly asked for it in writing. It's as simple as that.

There has to be no reference to unbearable suffering?

Yes, certainly. The Dutch rule is pretty good. There are about ten safeguards which I mentioned in my book. Suffering must be intolerable and there must be no cure for it. At least two doctors must agree on the decision to go ahead. Since I wrote that book I have been over to Holland and done a film about it, and one of the things which struck me forcibly was a charming woman GP we met who had helped three people to die. She said that when told that permission had been granted, two of them burst into tears and said, 'Thank you, thank you so much,' because they knew their suffering was going to be ended. That was quite impressive. Incidentally, many more requests for voluntary euthanasia in Holland are refused than granted.

One final question concerns the development of a euthanasia mentality. When David Steel introduced his bill on abortion in 1967, he had no idea that it would lead to an 'abortion on demand' mentality. Won't euthanasia go the same way?

There is a slight difference. Although abortion is much easier now, murder is still murder, and I think it is very unlikely that you will find doctors practising euthanasia in that loose way without permission and without consulting other doctors. I don't think there is the same danger.

Dame Cicely Saunders

Biographical details

Cicely Saunders is the founder of the modern-day hospice movement, having established St Christopher's Hospice in Sydenham in 1967, becoming its Medical Director.

Since then she has pioneered the development of palliative medicine, the speciality associated with hospice care both in this country and abroad. Her struggle has established a movement which now boasts over two hundred hospices and numerous homecare teams in the United Kingdom. Palliative medicine is now accepted as a medical discipline in its own right, with healthcare professionals having regular training in its techniques.

Her pioneering work has won her numerous honours including honorary fellowships from Cambridge and Yale. She won the Templeton Foundation Prize in 1981 and was awarded the Order of Merit in 1989. She has written numerous papers and publications regarding terminal care management.

Cicely Saunders has been highly acclaimed by many for the work she has pioneered. Polly Toynbee, the well-known columnist, writing in the *Guardian*, stated: 'She has changed the face of death for millions of people.' Her significance in the current euthanasia debate should not be underestimated. One leading medical peer was heard to say that if it wasn't for Cicely Saunders the United Kingdom would have had euthanasia years ago.

Cicely Saunders remains very active in the work of the hospice movement, and continues to live and work at St Christopher's Hospice in Sydenham.

Introductory comments

The impact of Cicely Saunders' pioneering work on the euthanasia debate, both in this country and abroad, should not be underestimated.

Before she began her work, only limited research had been undertaken on pain and developing new techniques for relieving it. There was a widespread fear of strong palliatives and the long-term impact upon patients. Practitioners were concerned about how much morphine and other palliatives patients could take before they became addicted. It was a common claim of those who advocated euthanasia that society was willing to put a dog out of its misery but not a loved one or fellow human being, and it was an argument which resonated with public opinion. However, the advances in pain relief pioneered by the hospice movement have been largely responsible for shifting the debate away from the key argument of pain and on to issues of autonomy and dignity.

The advances in pain relief have been unreservedly welcomed, but the hospice experiment has not been without its critics. For some time, hospices were stigmatised as places where people go to die. In fact, statistics from St Christopher's reveal this not to be the case, with the vast majority of patients dying at home. This, of course, is most people's preferred option. In addition, palliative care has had to fight to be recognised as a medical discipline in its own right. A rather ambivalent attitude was prevalent for a long time among many practitioners and is perhaps one reason for the general ignorance among the medical profession of the advances that have been made. For many years palliative medicine was not considered a medical speciality, and leading figures within the hospice movement campaigned for a long time to have it included as part of medical training.

Apart from these problems, hospice doctors have been accused of shortening the lives of their patients through large dosages of morphine, which is tantamount to euthanasia. Hospice doctors state that their intention is to relieve the pain, and they act within the boundaries of the principle of double effect, but some critics merely see this as a convenient screen hiding their real intentions. Further criticism has been levelled that they are only able to relieve the pain of 96 per cent of patients, and that the availability of hospice care is very patchy throughout the UK. Advocates of euthanasia have stated that voluntary euthanasia should be an option for the small but significant minority of patients whose suffering cannot be adequately relieved.

This interview seeks to secure answers to some of these contentious points. While refuting the charge of hypocrisy, Cicely Saunders stands firmly by the advances that have been made in the relief of pain. She recognises the need for further research and greater dissemination of the latest techniques, although she believes that a significant start has already been made.

Cicely Saunders is emphatic in her opposition to euthanasia. She cannot reconcile the practice with her understanding of the role of healthcare professionals, and is strongly opposed to it for social reasons. Despite having religious convictions, she does not discuss them, preferring to state her opposition to a change in law on social, medical and legal grounds. Her understanding of the practical problems involved reveals the extent of her clinical experience, caring for many in desperate need. Cicely Saunders' opposition also reveals the depth of the holistic approach which is so characteristic of hospice care. It is an approach whose impact is being increasingly felt within the care offered in the National Health Service.

It is her comments regarding the situation in the Netherlands which are likely to arouse the most interest. She refuses to accept the Dutch argument that their excellent old people's homes warrant hospices unnecessary. She accuses them of misunderstanding the basic proposal that a hospice is not a building, but more a philosophy. She admits that the Dutch geriatric provision is highly commendable, but states it is not designed to cope with those suffering from acute terminal illness. The administrative structure of a old people's home has a different style of management from the hospice and cannot react to the same needs. Her prediction of the future regarding the practice of euthanasia in the Netherlands will not be welcome news for those opposed to a change in law in the United Kingdom.

As with Ludovic Kennedy, Cicely Saunders continues to be a 'big' character who has been at the centre of the euthanasia debate for many years. Despite being over eighty she continues to be a highly influential figure in the future development of hospice care. It is unlikely that she will ever retire from her life's work and, whatever the outcome of the ongoing euthanasia debate, her tireless efforts on behalf of the sick and dying will be remembered for many years to come.

Interview

Can we begin by clarifying what is the impact of pain-relieving drugs on hospice patients in advanced stages of cancer or other diseases? Some say that by increasing pain relief you are shortening the patient's life. They accuse hospice doctors of acting hypocritically, shortening the life of the patient but not admitting it. Is this the case in your experience?

It is difficult to kill anyone with morphine. They tend to have a good sleep and then wake up again. If you want to kill someone you don't use morphine. You use potassium chloride or you do what they do in the Netherlands, according to the recent film *Death on Request*, where they gave morphine intravenously first and then gave a muscle relaxant. It's the relaxant and the potassium chloride that kill. The only way of killing with morphine is if a patient had not been having morphine, who was morphine naive, and was then given a very big dose. You might then do it, but in the story that they're talking about, about hospices and about escalating doses, (a) it doesn't happen and (b) if it did it probably wouldn't kill the patient anyway.

So what's the highest dose of morphine you have used here at St Christopher's? Something in the region of 25–30 milligrams every twelve hours is a figure I have heard.

I don't know where you have got that figure from. Each dose is individually calibrated, so there is no regular maximum. You can work up tolerance if you set out to do it, but of course you don't. You don't have problems with tolerance if you use drugs properly.

So from the type of drug used and the dose involved, it would appear that hospice doctors cannot be killing their patients. How do you react to charges of hypocrisy, that the hospice movement are hiding behind the principle of double effect, practising euthanasia but just not willing to admit it?

That's completely a story concocted by the Voluntary Euthanasia Society that simply isn't true, and we have chapter and verse to show that the level of doses that we were giving right up until 1984 were, for the vast majority, the dose you would give post-operatively or less. The small number needing a bigger dose is extremely limited. We are currently calculating the latest figures.

I think that the principle of double effect is much more likely to come into action with terminal restlessness than terminal pain. There's a paper in a recent *Journal of Palliative Medicine* which considered a group of patients, something like a hundred between St Joseph's Hospice and the London Hospital. The survey recorded that 23 per cent of the St Joseph's patients and 16 per cent of the London Hospital's had sedation before they died, which was for restlessness, delirium or whatever you like to call it, and the length of time they lived after sedation was one to three days – i.e. they weren't being given something that would knock them out straight away nor were they trailing on day after day after day. It was a controlled dose to control the restlessness which is so upsetting to the family, other patients and possibly to the patients themselves.

So there have been papers, and people have looked at it.

Do you think that one of the reasons there might be some confusion is because those who say it's hypocrisy don't really understand symptom control and the holistic aspect of hospice care?

Yes, I think they tend to imagine that all we're doing is giving drugs for pain. That's not true. It's a holistic look at the whole spectrum of symptoms, and if you deal with other symptoms you have less problem with pain. It is also looking at the emotional and mental pain, family pain and spiritual pain – looking at the patient as a whole person. In that context the times that you are really seriously looking at acting within the confines of the principle of double effect are very rare.

I remember talking to one hospice doctor who said the pain he found most difficult to control was that of a woman of thirty-five who was dying of cancer and leaving behind four children. It wasn't actually the physical disease that was causing the pain but the acute horrendous anxiety of leaving behind four children.

I absolutely agree. From experience here, pain is a very multifaceted thing, and somebody who has unfulfilled responsibilities like a young family is likely to have every-thing escalated. Some others will complain of pain because it's a respectable thing to complain of as compared with, 'I'm just miserable'; it's easier to say, 'I've got a bad pain.'

Looking at the wider issue of hospice care of which you are the founder, when did it actually all come into being, or is it something that's continuing to develop and you're finding new angles to it?

Well, it's both. We opened here at St Christopher's in 1967 by which time I had done seven years' work at St Joseph's introducing the regular giving of oral opiates, which was like waving a wand over the house, both because I was able to sit and talk to patients and had time, but mostly because of the change from people 'earning' their morphine by having pain first to putting them on to the regular morphine, which is enormously important.

What I was able to show in the first presentation for the Royal Society of Medicine in 1962, when I already had 900 analysed cases, was that we had no drug tolerance, no drug dependence and that we were using comparatively small doses. That was published in the beginning of 1963, so it dates right back to then, to my days at St Joseph's.

During the eight or so years before we opened here I did endless networking. I talked to lots of pain researchers and I analysed 1,100 patients' notes at St Joseph's and read what there was in the literature. Ever since 1967 we've been conducting research and we've been learning the whole time, so what we're doing now, thirty years later, is considerably more sophisticated. The basics remain the same, but we know much more about family anguish and spiritual pain, quite apart from all the physical nuances, nerve pain and so on, and if we're not doing better ten years ahead from now we'll be jolly bad. It's a continuing learning curve.

Back in the 1950s, what was terminal care like then? Were there many people dying in pain which could now be readily alleviated?

There are two studies, the Marie Curie Foundation Study through district nurses published in 1952, which showed an enormous amount of pain at home, and Professor John Hinton's first paper, 'The Physical and Mental Distress of the Dying', published in 1963. It studied 102 matched pairs of patients, 102 who died and 102 who were seriously ill but didn't die, and it showed again physical distress, pain, breathlessness, and so on. That study remains probably the most detailed study which has ever been done. Those were the sort of studies, added to my own, that I was able to present to people when I was raising the money to build St Christopher's and persuaded the Nuffield Foundation and the City Parochial Foundation and others to give us the money to build. We had to research and teach.

Was there any understanding of palliative care in those days?

No, the word 'palliative' wasn't about, apart from palliative radiotherapy. There was no special way of looking after the dying. It was left to the nurses. People were written up for having painkillers and they used what they called the Brompton Cocktail, which came from the Brompton Chest Hospital. It was written as four-hourly PRN, that is 'if necessary', so it was never given until the patient had pain first, and pain is the strongest antagonist to anything that you're going to give to control it. So the simple method of giving regularly four-hourly before pain happened, which I met as a volunteer in St Luke's Hospital from 1948 onwards, and which I introduced to St Joseph's in 1958, was in a sense a revolution. It was there but it hadn't been published, it hadn't been researched. As a result, a lot of people with cancer were having really bad pain and the fear was that patients would become addicted, drug dependent, and people would be told, 'See if you can hold on a little longer,' so that they had to earn their morphine over and over again.

What medical students were taught about was what I often call 'Teaching Hospital Pain'. This is post-operative, post-burn, post-trauma, events with a built-in meaning and an end time-scale. In such circumstances to have drugs for pain when you get pain is pretty logical. But the chronic pain which goes on the whole time wasn't seen in teaching hospitals anything like so much, so doctors were coming into practice and behaving as though it was acute pain when it was really constant pain needing constant control. As a result they were approaching a patient's need in a totally inappropriate way.

You have obviously made significant developments in techniques in relieving pain and yet you are accused by some of being only able to secure relief in 96 per cent of cases. Doesn't this warrant euthanasia as a necessary option for the 4 per cent you cannot help?

If somebody who is terminally ill is prepared to accept sedation, nobody need die in pain. If they are not prepared to accept sedation then we may have people who continue to complain, but on the whole they aren't the ones who are asking for euthanasia. By sedation I mean making them sleepy, and there are different levels of sedation. Occasionally a really confused, delirious patient may have to be kept unconscious the whole time. I repeat, nobody need die in pain, but the occasional one who won't accept sedation may have a rough passage. However, the 4 per cent are not necessarily the ones who are asking for euthanasia. Of the patients who are in the 4 per cent bracket, they often feel restlessness rather than pain. Pain when people move can be quite difficult pain to control, so if you prevent movement they don't get the pain, and of course when they're terribly ill they aren't likely to move anyway and nursing has to be especially skilled.

When you began your work one of the main arguments in favour of euthanasia obviously was pain. Is it the case now?

It's dependence more now, and it was dependence then as well. A lack of control over what's happening, being dependent, 'I'm going to lose my dignity, I'm going to be incontinent, I'm going to lose my marbles,' and so on and so forth. However, in answer to your question, just because we are having some success in preventing pain doesn't mean that everybody does it, so we are left with a huge education problem which we have been working on over the years.

In terms of the dissemination of knowledge and good practice, what have you achieved in the last thirty years?

There are now over two hundred centres of hospice care and thousands of homecare nurses in the UK and some eighty places around the world. I wrote in 1959 in a series of articles in the *Nursing Times* that those of us who are opposed to euthanasia have the right to say so, but also the responsibility of doing something about it, which I've been doing ever since. It's quite a long time now, and I still remain opposed to euthanasia primarily for social reasons.

I don't deny that there are some people who are not getting optimum care, that there are some people who like to have a control over their lives; with some there may be a big fear of dying and they think they could control it by having euthanasia. For some there is the fear of losing dignity and not being, as it were, in sync with the rest of their lives. However, I don't think that this minority, and I believe it is a minority, can have a legal right to a quick out without undermining the majority who simply want good care and aren't going to ask for euthanasia.

You mentioned the loss of dignity. Wouldn't you say that what you are practising here is an attempt to bring dignity to the end of life?

Yes, I spent ten years looking after my husband and for the last four years he was pretty heavy to move. I remember one night when we were getting him on to the commode how the friend who was helping me said, 'You know, he's lost his modesty but he's kept his dignity.' It is quite possible to keep your dignity when you are going on to a commode if the attitude of the people around you is such that they are seeing you as a person still having worth.

If the minority were to have their way and euthanasia were legalised, what effect do you think that would have, first, on what you have achieved already, and second, what you will achieve in the next thirty years?

People say there would be no more money for research and palliative care but I don't know if I really go along with that. There might not be so much interest because there would be a lot of people who would say, 'Why are you prolonging life for people when, really, look at them! And look at the National Opinion Poll, 70–80 per cent of people say doctors should be able to end suffering quickly.' What I think is that an awful lot of people would say, 'I'm nothing but a burden and I ought to opt out,' and would miss the sort of thing that my husband got three hours before he died, which was thanks for his life's work from the son of another patient. I've seen people over many years who've only reached the reconciliation, the thanks, the quietness, at the end, when they might have got out beforehand with bitterness and pain and left behind very sad memories. We know that bereavement after suicide is a particularly difficult bereavement to come to terms with, and I personally think the bereavement after euthanasia could be very much the same. But I also agree that the bereavement after unrelieved pain is very difficult to come to terms with, and that's our commitment.

Do you think it is possible to attend a hospice and have as one option symptom control management, and the other option a hospice doctor injecting you with potassium chloride when the family and everyone's discussed it?

This has been discussed a great deal in the States, especially in Oregon, and it's a complete change of direction which I think any palliative care doctor that I know of in this country wouldn't find acceptable at all. You can't suddenly kill someone who you've been caring for, because it goes absolutely against your reason for coming into medicine. There was a very good article in a past *Journal of Palliative Medicine* saying that, were euthanasia to be legalised, doctors should never be involved with it, it should be two lawyers and a technician. It's not very difficult to kill someone by injecting potassium chloride.

Imagine the people that you're caring for and deciding that this is the day that you're going to end it. Imagine the patient trying to decide which day. They couldn't, because they do change their minds, to and fro. The ones who are asking now are not usually very consistent, so how are we to decide for them if they can't decide for themselves?

You don't think you could have a technician attached to St Christopher's who did that sort of work?

That answers itself as you ask it!

Looking at the experience in the Netherlands, could you explain your own involvement with current medical practice in the Netherlands and whether or not your advice has been sought?

I've met Dr Zylicz and there's an article by him on my desk at the moment, where another Dutch doctor wanted a hospital bed and just simply put an end to the patient's life. We did have a Dutch nurse at St Christopher's for three months whose uncle had motor neurone disease. He didn't want euthanasia, but twice had people asking him if he wanted it. When he said 'no' they admitted him to hospital and he had a lousy last year.

We had another doctor who spent his holiday in the Netherlands and met up with an old friend who was nursing there. In her ward was a patient with leukaemia who at a weekend said, 'I'm tired of this, I'd like euthanasia now.' The doctor on duty had never seen the patient before; he rang up the consultant who said, 'That's all right, you can go ahead,' and he did. So all they say about guidelines may be true for what the doctors report back to the questionnaires, but there must be quite a lot going on otherwise. The palliative care practice in the Netherlands is only developing. It is very telling that the House of Lords Select Committee were finally decided by their visit to the Netherlands. They believed that the line between voluntary and involuntary euthanasia was impossible to draw.

Do you think there is any correlation between the fact that they have euthanasia and they have very little in the way of hospice services? Have you tried to disseminate information there?

I've left it to others. I think it's safer to say 'palliative care' in Europe because 'hospice' isn't such an acceptable word. People do so much think of hospice as bricks and mortar and don't realise that most of our patients are at home anyway. I have been told that the Minister for Health was very moved by the discussion which Dr Sykes and I joined after the film *Death on Request.*

The Dutch have a very well-funded system of old people's homes and they claim this is their alternative to hospice care.

It is right, they claim they don't need it because they look at some of our geriatric services and say they are appalling in comparison to their own services. Yes, but those elderly homes have waiting lists and are not there for the acute crisis of people dying of cancer. In such circumstances you need an easily available bed, and a long-term nursing home has very slow turnover. Such homes are not an answer to the euthanasia problem.

Only recently a group of nursing home superintendents from the Netherlands visited St Christopher's to see what palliative care in Britain was really all about. It is really a different scene with very different staff ratios.

If an individual contracted cancer in the UK they could be referred to a hospice, but in the Netherlands they would not be able to go to an old people's home because they would not qualify, for obvious reasons. The Dutch would go to their GP, but there would be little advice available in terms of specialist palliative care.

Your GP could ring Dr Zylicz in Arnhem Hospice for advice.

One doctor in the whole of the country?

Well, there are probably some others now, but he runs a service of giving advice.

And that would be it?

Well, just about. Dr Zylicz is about the only doctor working in it full time to my understanding. So it is not easy to find. Incidentally, he followed me round Poland as a Polish medical student when I was lecturing there in 1978 and translated my small book. He then moved to the Netherlands, worked in oncology and was so horrified by what he saw that he went on and specialised and got himself into palliative medicine. So he is another off-shoot from experience here, rather indirectly.

Do you think in the light of the Remmelink Report that there might come a time when the Dutch actually turn their backs on euthanasia?

I should think that it's pretty unlikely. By comparison, is there any chance of stepping back from abortion on demand, which is not what the 1967 Act was meant to produce? We are never going to step back. There is the 'altered standpoint' that Bernard Levin has written about. Once you've got an altered standpoint among the public you are not going to change things. If they ever legalised euthanasia here, it would never go back again, and in the same way I don't think they'd ever go back in the Netherlands.

Considering there are approximately a thousand cases of non-voluntary euthanasia each year, don't you think that the Dutch penal code is failing to protect its citizens and to uphold the country's duty as a signatory of the European Convention of Human Rights?

It is not my particular expertise, but I think that Dutch doctors would say that these are patients within a few days of death, who would have asked anyway, and whose pain was difficult to control, and so on.

Do you consider the continued practice of euthanasia in the Netherlands a threat to what you are doing in this country?

I think it is a warning, and I think that is what the House of Lords Select Committee concluded. It hasn't been so far. It has been going on a long time, and for all the pro-euthanasia lobby pressure, it hasn't persuaded the law-givers and it didn't persuade the House of Lords, who were not all on one side when they started out. But there is much inaccurate media reporting which confuses the issues. I mean, the report on Baroness Warnock's husband's death and what the GP did was ridiculous. It was not euthanasia, it was good care. Having said that, the trouble is some inexperienced doctors do not really know treatment from euthanasia, and so reporting becomes very problematic. I think the Dutch experience will be damaging in the sense that the more it's talked about the more the general public will look over and see that Holland does not seem to fall apart as a country. They see it is still all there and the Dutch look as happy as they ever did, and it doesn't really seem to do them any harm, so what is wrong with it? I think it is going to be damaging in that way, really.

What is interesting is the view of the general public. Although the VES-commissioned NOP poll said that 70–80 per cent are in favour, Julia Addington Hall's study, the regional study of dying, *The Year Before Death*, showed that in 24 per cent of the cases where they said they would have liked to have died sooner, only 3.6 per cent actually asked for euthanasia. I know this relies on the memory of the carers, but even so, even if you, say, double it, it is still a very small figure, and that is what the people at the end of their lives are actually saying.

Would you describe yourself as a supporter of advance directives?

I have told my own GP the things that I am not prepared to have done and I have let my family know, but I didn't write out a full advance directive. I think people should think ahead. Whether it should have any more legal force than it has got at the moment, I am not so sure. What you cannot have in an advance directive is to ask someone to do something that is illegal, and as long as you are very sure about that, it may help. I think it probably should be just part of the evidence that a doctor looks at when he is considering decisions for an unconscious patient. A directive can be a help for the doctor when discussing with the family and the others. But I know the pro-life movement are very against advance directives and the voluntary euthanasia movement are very much in favour. I think it depends entirely on what you put in it.

So you would be against legislation promoting legally binding advance directives?

Well, I wouldn't stand up and die for it, whereas I might against voluntary euthanasia!

Baroness Warnock

Biographical details

Baroness Warnock is one of the UK's leading ethicists, renowned for her work in many of the complex ethical areas facing medicine.

A former Mistress of Girton College, Cambridge, she has been chairman of numerous committees focusing on key ethical questions. Among others, she served on the Royal Commission on Environmental Pollution and chaired the Advisory Committee on Animal Experimentation. Her work as Chairman of the Committee of Inquiry into Human Fertilisation during the 1980s received considerable public acclaim and paved the way for legislation on embryo research.

Baroness Warnock has written numerous papers and books on philosophy and ethics and is a frequent contributor to many radio and television broadcasts. In recognition of her work she has gained many honorary degrees from universities around the world.

Baroness Warnock was a member of the House of Lords Select Committee on Medical Ethics.

Introductory comments

An assessment of the current euthanasia debate would be incomplete without considering the views of Baroness Warnock. Her influence in matters medical remains significant, yet in the euthanasia debate both sides have privately 'boasted' that they enjoy her support. The fact that she was a signatory to the House of Lords Select Committee on Medical Ethics is seen by those against euthanasia as a sign of her support. At the same time, those who advocate a change in law state her dissatisfaction with the current legal framework as an indication of where her thinking lies.

The interview clarifies her position, showing that while she was in favour of change prior to the Medical Ethics Select Committee, her views changed under the influence of some legal arguments during the Committee. Rather than advocating a change in law legalising euthanasia, Baroness Warnock is a strong supporter of reforming the mandatory life sentence for murder. This would enable judges to take into account the motive, should a doctor be charged with the murder of his or her patient. Baroness Warnock explains clearly her reasons for advocating such a change.

A further important area which is explored during the interview concerns the actions of doctors under the principle of double effect. Baroness Warnock launches a scathing attack on its use, describing it as a 'double deception', with doctors 'fudging the facts'. Baroness Warnock finds the principle morally objectionable, but acknowledges that it works effectively in practice and so advocates the law remaining as it is.

Turning to a further legal point, Baroness Warnock assesses the legal arguments surrounding the Bland judgment and its implications for the euthanasia debate. She attacks the attempts to distinguish between medical treatment and nursing care, stating that in truth a value judgment had to be made about Tony Bland. She believes that it is more honest to make such value judgments than to look for other 'fatuous' legal arguments to justify the withdrawal of food and fluid. Baroness Warnock states that 'the life of a human is more than just being alive'. She outlines her adherence to this view and gives an insight of how we should care for those suffering from Alzheimer's and motor neurone disease, and the mentally ill.

Throughout, she states clearly her position on the issue of euthanasia. However, both sides of the debate will find some encouragement in the views of Baroness Warnock as expressed in the interview and may continue to see her as a sympathetic if not an ardent supporter.

Interview

You were a member of the House of Lords Select Committee on Medical Ethics and signed the unanimous report stating that there should be no change in law with regard to euthanasia. Is that still your view?

I signed the report, but I think there are quite a number of things which need to be clarified within the law. There were three of us, all women, who started off absolutely certain that we wanted a change in the law – Baroness Llewelyn Davies, who has now died, Baroness Jay and me. We were actually won over not by the doctors but by the lawyers, particularly Lord Mustill, who had been one of the judges considering the Tony Bland case. I think our only positive recommendation was that the mandatory sentence for murder should be changed and it should lie with a judge to recommend what sentence he thought suitable. Some Committee members objected to that on the grounds that they thought it should be a medical decision, not a legal one. I dissent from that. I think it ought to be a legal decision.

What are your reasons for thinking that the mandatory life sentence for murder needs to be changed?

It seems to me there are circumstances in which a doctor or a relative might be charged with murder, but where the motive for murder, as opposed to the intention, would be so benign that the judge would wish not to impose a life sentence. At present a life sentence is very harsh. I researched the Parole Board figures, and it turns out that nobody who's been convicted of that kind of murder has served less than six years. So it's a very, very harsh sentence.

Rather than changing the law, would it not be better for a judge to consider whether the doctor acted in the best interests of a patient and on the persistent request of a patient, and apply a more lenient sentence if appropriate?

That's more or less what I think I'm after. If such a case came to court at all it would be tried as a case of murder because it was intentional killing; but it should be open to the judge to give a very lenient sentence or none at all.

Would this in effect be a new law called 'mercy killing'?

No. It is intentional killing, and so would always have to be a case of murder. What one needs to do is to distinguish the intention from the motive, and a judge is capable of doing this on hearing the facts. So if he heard that the relatives and the patient had expressed themselves and were really extremely anxious for the death of the patient, then the motive of the doctor would be to make the death as easy as possible. The intention would still be to bring about death, or hasten it. The difficulty comes not in the case of terminal illness but in the case in which somebody is not terminally but irreversibly ill, and doesn't want to go on living. I think that's a much more difficult case. It's quite easy to see when someone is going to die anyway within a week or month or so; and easing the passing is not a tremendous crime – in fact it may not be a moral crime at all, even though it's intentional killing. But to take the life of someone who has perhaps years to live may seem more morally dubious.

I'm interested that you don't support the mercy-killing argument for a new law.

I think it would produce exactly the same problems under another name. One would still have problems with definition. You might as well stick with a charge of murder for which there would be exonerating circumstances, rather than introduce a new category of 'mercy killing', which would be very grey at the edges. It would have to be looked at by the law in every individual case, otherwise it could so easily be abused.

The House of Lords Select Committee Report stated that the prohibition of intentional killing is a cornerstone of the current law, a boundary which it would be very wrong for society to cross.

I quite agree with that, and that was why I signed the report. It was the basis of Lord Mustill's argument on that Committee. I think it would be widely agreed by a great many judges that once one gave it up, all kinds of activities could creep in, with a damaging effect on society.

You don't think, if your suggested change occurred and judges passed a number of lenient judgments, you would in effect have legalised euthanasia? Doctors would see that a reasonable body of legal opinion had been established which exonerated the practice.

I think you probably would, but only in certain very specific circumstances. It would still entail that in every other case doctors could face being challenged, even though they might feel fairly secure that they would win in court. It is rather different from the current position in the Netherlands.

Dutch physicians state that the problem with the current law is that they have to criminalise themselves and so the onus is on the doctor, which could result in a prison sentence.

This seems to me a position the law wouldn't accept here. It's a very, very peculiar position for the doctors to be in.

Can I explore further the principle of double effect. There seems to be considerable confusion as to what it exactly means. I read in a recent paper of one professor who equates double effect with intentional killing. Others understand the principle of double effect to be the foreseen but unintended effect of shortening life. They suggest that there is an element of doubt as to whether or not what you are doing will result in shortening the life. The House of Lords Select Committee took this view. Perhaps you could explain how you view the principle?

The thing that's wrong with the argument of double effect is that it pretends to be able to distinguish among our intentions long term and immediate, in a way we in fact don't do in real life. The argument which makes me feel the appeal to double effect is so shifty is precisely the argument that the doctors don't know what the effect of, say, increasing the dose of morphia is going to be. But if they say they don't know that, then they ought to say they don't know all kinds of other things, namely that morphia will make breathing easier. It is absurd to say that the criterion for knowledge is so strict that they can say, 'I know this will give you a good night's sleep,' but 'I don't know that it will ultimately hasten your death.' But that is the argument many doctors rely on because they think it will let them off the hook.

Of course, things might intervene that were unforeseen, but your intention nevertheless would be unchanged. One example I have given in the past is that I'm standing at the table putting bits of cutlery around, and you say, 'What are you doing?' and I could say, 'I'm putting a fork on the left of the table mat,' or I could say, 'I'm laying the table,' or I could say, 'I'm preparing for my dinner party.' If I say that the last, which describes the whole of what I'm intending, is what I am doing, then of course there could be a bomb and the house might blow up and I might not have a dinner party. But I don't take that possibility into account when I tell you what I'm intentionally doing.

Doctors I have discussed the issue with suggest that the drugs being used can reveal the doctor's intention. In any case, it is notoriously difficult to kill patients with palliatives because often you are dealing with patients who have become dependent on such drugs and an increase is unlikely to shorten life. They say that reveals their intention.

Some doctors feel confident that they have no intention except to ease suffering. So be it. But then they've got to say, 'Unfortunately, by accident the patient died rather sooner than he probably would have.' If they know their business, they know that this very often happens, but the patient is in a reasonably happy condition and he would in any case have only a few days or weeks longer to live. The doctors have made a value judgment, but I think they are unwilling to admit it. The doctors on the House of Lords Select Committee were very unwilling to admit this; but in fact they are saying to themselves that the most important thing is to relieve the suffering and it doesn't matter very much if the patient dies. That's why terminally ill cases are so easy – you know the patient's going to die anyway in the foreseeable future, and you can't prevent him from dying.

If you took away the principle of double effect and doctors weren't allowed to work within its parameters, then patients would be dying in pain because doctors would be fearful of increasing morphine. This would turn the clock back prior to Cicely Saunders' intervention in 1967.

The best-known case was that of Dr Bodkin Adams, and he was not convicted. The reason was that Lord Devlin, on his behalf, deployed the double effect argument. I'm sure the double effect argument has been used for years. It's a way of letting people conscientiously do things which they actually, in their heart of hearts, knew would have a forbidden effect. It was used frequently by Jesuits in the case of telling lies, which was forbidden. If you said something that was not exactly a lie, but was misleading, you could regard that misleading as an effect that happened although it was not what you intended. You intended to tell the truth.

So is your quarrel with it a moral or a legal one?

It's a moral one. It seems to me to be a ridiculous quibble to say that you are doing whatever you do without taking any account of the consequences. It's then a double deception to say not only that you're not taking account of the consequences, but that you don't know what the consequences will be. The fact is, they're fudging it: they have made a value judgment, namely that it is more important to ease the patient's suffering than to calculate whether or not he's going to die sooner.

Aren't you being morally purist?

I'm very glad that the argument from double effect has not been taken to exonerate doctors, even by the Vatican Council – and nobody could be more hard line. I'm extremely glad it works, and it has been deemed to be an effective method enabling doctors to do this kind of thing and get away with it. I still think it's somehow an objectionable feature of life that they are able to do this by a very defective argument. It's as if we've all conspired to use our arguments for our own purposes, which I'm all for, but I wish it wasn't quite so fudgy. Perhaps I'm a *logical* purist.

The pro-euthanasia lobby are very much against the use of double effect. They see it as a stumbling block to a change in the law. One physician interviewed described it as 'double effect death', 'pharmacological oblivion'. They attack the principle because it upholds the current legal position.

That's exactly what I want. I don't want a change in the law, though I do want the law to be clarified. If a doctor acts in a way to hasten his terminally ill patient's death, he will not be prosecuted. As I said, that is accepted by the Vatican Council and by most doctors now. And so it would be only if someone challenged the doctor that the argument of double effect would have to be deployed.

If you will accept the argument that doctors are knowingly shortening life under the guise of double effect, do you think that a doctor should be able to use potassium chloride as opposed to using opiates? If you're happy for the opiates to shorten life, why can't doctors use a poison?

This is one of the great troubles. If the patient wants to die and the family want him to die, why can't the doctor give him a lethal injection of whatever it may be? One obviously doesn't want the doctor to give a poison which will cause an agonising death, but there must be suitable poisons. The trouble is the doctor's caught in a situation where if he gives a lethal dose that will immediately cause death, that is quite obviously intentional killing and is murder. What he does if he gives an increased dose of morphia is to cause death *indirectly*, so to speak, and he can argue that he didn't intend the murder but he did intend the alleviation of suffering. As I have said, I don't believe in this argument's safety, but if it works let it work, because it makes for a good outcome.

Can we focus on the Bland judgment, because there seems to be considerable confusion in that area too. The case focuses partly on whether there is any difference between an act and an omission.

The distinction between acts of commission and acts of omission is based on an extraordinarily primitive notion of causation which wouldn't stand up to ordinary common sense. Obviously you can kill your cat by shooting it or by neglecting to feed it, but in either case you would be doing something that was equally morally reprehensible. In French law this is differently regarded. In English law if you push somebody into the canal and they drown, you have caused their death, whereas if you are a strong swimmer and walk past somebody in manifest difficulties drowning in the canal you are not guilty of anything. In France there is a law against this type of failure to rescue. The English law's built-in concept of cause is exceptionally primitive, and if you look at remarks judges tend to make about cause, they distinguish very sharply between what you do and what you omit.

Do you think the Bland judgment was non-voluntary euthanasia because there was a failure to feed him, just as you described in the incident with the cat?

There were so many complications in the Bland case. For instance, the House of Lords Select Committee got terribly hung up on the fatuous argument distinguishing between nursing care and medical treatment. That is an absolute absurdity, because if you start making that kind of distinction you've got to say whether feeding someone with a teaspoon is medical intervention or not. Bland was being fed and hydrated by methods that couldn't possibly have been used outside hospital, so it was part of his treatment that he was being kept alive. I think if one stopped using the expressions 'voluntary euthanasia' and 'involuntary euthanasia' it would be very much clearer. The word 'euthanasia' has so much baggage attached to it that I try to avoid using it at all. Again, I would rather say that in the case of Bland there was a value judgment made that a life such as he was leading was simply not something that had any value at all, to him, his relatives or anyone else. It was also very expensive to maintain. Therefore, one was judging that it was more important not to maintain life by feeding than to continue to maintain it. It was morally more important to let him off the hook than to keep him on it.

The people who would object to that moral judgment are the people who think that life itself is intrinsically valuable, whatever its quality. Those 'pro-lifers' would never be won over to the view that his life was worth nothing. But other people who are not 'pro-lifers' make the distinction between the life of a baby who's got no brain, for example, or Tony Bland, who is insensate, and other kinds of lives. There's no arguing with the 'pro-lifers' and you'll never get them to accept the death of Tony Bland. If you're not in this sense pro-life then you've got to make a value judgment; and in the end it seems to me that this turns on the safety of the diagnosis of PVS, on the wishes of the relatives and on the amount of resources that are being poured into keeping a PVS patient alive. It would have been perfectly possible for the Airedale Hospital to have said, 'This boy has PVS and will never recover. We can't afford to keep him alive, and if you, the relatives, wish to keep him alive then I'm afraid you have to pay for it.' That seems to me a moral judgment. They would be saying that there are other patients we could afford to treat if only we were not treating Bland. That would have been an honest way to go about it; but they didn't do that. Perhaps fearful of an outcry, understandably they took it to court.

I do think that to use expressions like 'voluntary' or 'involuntary euthanasia' immediately categorises the case in a particular way which may not exactly fit it. What is involuntary euthanasia? Is it euthanasia where the patient is in no state to express his wishes? Does it cover the case of the baby without a brain who is taken off the life-support machine? Is it meant for that or not?

Some have defined euthanasia as the intentional killing of a patient by act or omission as part of their medical treatment.

Withdrawal of life-support machines counts as euthanasia if this definition is correct. It must if it's intentional killing by act or omission, as part of the medical treatment.

It doesn't in that definition because the withdrawal of a life-support machine involves taking away a machine which is performing a function the body can no longer do by itself. However, with regard to food and water you are not withdrawing a machine which is performing the function of a failing organ but rather the sustenance all life needs to survive. That I understand is the distinction.

Then I think it is an absurd distinction. What's the difference between the blood being pumped round by some artificial outside agency and the hydration or nutrition being absorbed by the stomach through some outside agency, as in the case of Bland? There is no difference. In either case the functions of the body go on only because the machinery is working, and the patient will die without it, whether it's putting liquids or nutrition into the body or whether it's the pump that pumps the heart.

Others choose to argue that food is a basic human right which should not be removed except where the patient is close to death.

That's rubbish. It would be a human right only if the person has a right to live. What is this human right? You could say that the beating of the heart is a human right, or the activity of any of the cells of the body is a human right, in the sense that it would be depriving somebody of something if you stopped their heart beating.

Returning to some of the other questions raised by the Bland case, what criteria would you use to decide whether or not food and water should be withdrawn from patients in PVS? Should this practice be extended to patients in conditions other than PVS?

It needs a competent medical practitioner to say what a good diagnosis should be based on. Obviously it would be far safer in the case of PVS if there could be criteria for diagnosis which were based not so much on symptoms as on the condition of the brain. This was possible in the Bland case because his brain was found to be a mass of liquid. It was as certain as it could be that he would not recover, or that if he did make a partial recovery, his brain would be so severely damaged that his life would not be worth living. That last judgment can be made pretty securely on the knowledge of what, in the way of human functions, the different bits of the brain enable us to perform. So if you take a baby with no brain or almost no brain, you can tell absolutely securely that the quality of that baby's life, if it's allowed to live, will be hopeless. I think one needs to make it quite clear that such a baby would not be living in the way humans do live. If life alone was intrinsically valuable then one would have to go into mourning for every spermatozoon that didn't achieve fertilisation, because there's no doubt that spermatozoa are alive, just as eggs are alive. So if we're talking about life alone we'd be in a fairly bad state, with the waste all around us. But it isn't simply life, it's the life of a human being that we're interested in, and the life of a human being is more than just being alive. This would be my argument in favour of our being able to make these value judgments about what life is worth living.

If you have a patient with progressive Alzheimer's, whose life is manifestly horrible, I think there's a great difficulty, because people may feel great affection for those who are suffering from Alzheimer's and they can't contemplate themselves being the agent of their death. But if there were a drug which would make the life of an Alzheimer's patient less panicky and awful and terrifying, but would bring it about that their life was shortened, I think most doctors would fall back on the old double effect friend and use it, provided that the person who was looking after the victim would agree to the use of the drug. I think this is an area that is far more difficult than the Bland case, because the Alzheimer's patient is not terminally ill, and is not insensate either, but is suffering.

Isn't the problem that you can't make a distinction between those in PVS, those who are terminally ill and those suffering from Alzheimer's disease?

No. It is possible and necessary to make some distinctions. With PVS you know that the patient is not terminally ill, though he can feel nothing. He is not in pain or distress either. Bland could have been kept alive for thirty or forty years. The Bland case is a very different case from the sort of case we started with, where the patient only has weeks or possibly months to live, and is suffering. If the case is in the middle, which might include the Alzheimer's case, then I think it would be stretching 'terminally ill' to say that that person was terminal. And it is here that the difficulty about euthanasia principally arises. One cannot say that killing the Alzheimer's patient is 'easing the passing'.

What you are saying is that you have to make a value judgment on the basis of diagnosis for patients in PVS, and that value judgment says there is no quality of life. What if someone suffering from Alzheimer's or motor neurone disease, with a poor prognosis, repeatedly asked to die? The patient, doctor and the family could make a value judgment that life is really not worth living. Surely there is no moral distinction between the two cases? You accept it for PVS – why not for motor neurone disease?

I don't think there's any important moral distinction at all. There's no distinction between the Bland case and Annie Lindsell, except that she was instrumental (or hoped to be) in deciding what life was and was not worth living. I think she was taking for herself the judgment the judges took in the Bland case; and she brought it to court in order to be sure that her doctor would not be led into criminalising himself if he gave her the fatal dose when she judged that her life was intolerable. It was a very important case because it does align the Bland case with the motor neurone case, and Alzheimer's could perhaps be viewed the same way, except that the judgment as to when life became valueless there would have to be made by another person. What was interesting to me about the Annie Lindsell case was that people said there was no reason to bring it to court, in that the doctor would have been acting within the law if he had given her a death-hastening dose when her illness had progressed to the acute stage. I would like to see this further explored so that the law could be clear.

There was a heated debate in the House of Lords regarding the case tabled by Lord Lester, who was counsel to Annie Lindsell.

Lord Lester's defence seemed very good, and also Stephen Brown's judgment in the case, which I think ought to be written up in gold. What I think does harm the issue is the use of the word 'euthanasia'. People immediately take up pre-formed positions about it, without looking at the issues involved in each particular kind of case.

Do you think that ultimately the debate over euthanasia will fall back on whether a person believes in the sanctity of life? Thirty years ago the big argument was, 'You put a dog out of its pain, why not a human being?' But the hospice movement has done a considerable amount in advancing the relief of pain. Now the debate appears to be moving on to issues of dignity and personal choice.

I think there is no argument with the people who have as their first principle and dogma that all life is *equally* sacred. Those people are never going to accept the necessity for intentionally depriving somebody of life. What I find very limiting is that the palliative medicine lobby tend to concentrate entirely on pain and they don't talk about other conditions which are conditions of acute distress. Nor do they recognise that, excellent though the hospice movement is, both in hospice and at home, there are still many people for whom palliative care is inadequate.